Planning Good Change
with Technology
and Literacy

by Jamie McKenzie

FNO Press
Bellingham, Washington
http://fnopress.com

FNO Press http://fnopress.com

This work contains articles previously published in a number of journals and publications.

"Pacing Change" first appeared as an article in **Connected Classroom**.

"The Unplugged Classroom," "Beware the Wizard," "Network Starvation," and "Making Good Change" first appeared as columns in **eSchool News**.

"How Teachers Learn Best" was first published in **The Electronic School**.

"Beyond IT," "The New New Thing," "Beware the Shallow Waters," "What's the Story Here?" "Strategic Deployment," "The Research Gap," "Waste Not, Want Not," and "Managing Quandaries" appeared first as articles in **From Now On**.

Making Good Change is dedicated to students who dare to ask essential questions, challenge conventional wisdom, and create good new ideas.

In addition, this book is dedicated to teachers who recognize the passionate flight of such students as the ultimate reward of teaching.

Finally, these pages are dedicated to planners who refuse to put the cart before the horse - who stand firmly instead against fads and bandwagons while prizing literacy over gadgetry and gimmickry.

About the author . . .

Jamie McKenzie is the Editor of **From Now On - The Educational Technology Journal**, a Web-based zine published since 1991. In this journal he has argued for information literate schools. More than twenty-five per cent of his 21,000+ subscribers live in countries outside of North America such as Australia, New Zealand, Sweden, Malaysia and Singapore.

From 1993-1997, Jamie was the Director of Libraries, Media and Technology for the Bellingham (WA) Public Schools, a district of 19 schools and 10,000 students that was fully networked with 2000 desktops all tied to the Internet in 1995. He has since moved on to support literacy, technology planning, and professional development across North America, Australia and New Zealand.

A graduate of Yale with an M.A. from Columbia and Ed.D. from Rutgers, Jamie has been a middle school teacher of English and social studies, an assistant principal, an elementary principal, an assistant superintendent in Princeton (NJ), and a superintendent of two districts on the East coast of the States. He also taught four-year-olds in Sunday school.

Jamie has published and spoken extensively on the introduction of new technologies to schools. In recent times, he has paid particular attention to information technologies and how they might transform classrooms and schools to support student-centered, engaged learning.

A full resume listing publication credits and a detailed career history is available online at http://fno.org/JM/resume.html.

Introduction

Despite huge expenditures on the installation of networked computers throughout classrooms globally , we have very little credible evidence that this activity has improved student skills or performance.

This book - **Making Good Change** - is offered to focus the planning process on something much more important than networking and connectivity:

Literacy and Student Learning

Given the attention devoted to school restructuring in the previous decade, it may seem peculiar to focus so much attention upon student learning when schools are thinking about technology. But this book will argue that technology is mainly a delivery system for something far more important - a curriculum that is standards-based, vigorous, and engaging.

This book maintains that it is wrong-minded and shortsighted to make technology, networking, and connectivity the goal.

The first two books of this series showed how schools might take advantage of networks to raise a generation of **free range students** – young people capable of navigating through a complex, often disorganized information landscape while making up their own minds about the important issues of their lives and their times. This kind of thinking - interpreting, reasoning, and understanding - we might call **literacy.** The skills required to achieve literacy across a dozen types of information will serve young people well on Life's tests as well as on the increasingly challenging state tests.

An essential step toward forming an engaging, effective program is to think of students as *infotectives*.

What is an *infotective*? . . . a student thinker capable of asking great questions about data in order to convert the *data* into *information* and eventually into *insight* (information that may suggest action or strategy of some kind.)

An *infotective* solves information puzzles with a combination of inference skills and new technologies. An *infotective* is a skilled thinker, researcher, and inventor.

Infotective is a term designed for education in an Age of Information. In the smokestack school, teachers imparted meanings for students to digest, memorize, and regurgitate. In Information Age schools, students make the meaning. They puzzle their way through piles of fragments - sorting, sifting, weighing, and arranging them until a picture emerges.

Literacy!

Literacy skills are likely to produce improved performance on the increasingly challenging state tests of reading comprehension and problem solving. As state standards require more and more inferential reasoning, state tests are asking students to "create answers" rather than "find answers."

The planning process that creates *infotectives* begins with classroom issues and challenges rather than wires and cables. The school that puts curriculum and learning first will not fall prey to the current trend of putting the "cart before the horse." Once the learning goals and activities are clear, and only then, can the network designers begin to create the technological support that teachers, librarians and principals request for their students and families.

This book argues that educators should direct this design process to serve curriculum goals, **literacy** . . . and students!

Contents

Chapter 1 - Making Good Change

It is easy to make change.
Change happens.
Even if we sit still . . . do nothing . . . change happens.
It is more difficult to make **good** change.
Change that makes life better. Change that endures.
Change that persists.

Making good change in schools is much more challenging than most policy makers and outsiders seem to understand.

We have decades of excellent research studies identifying which change strategies work and which fail. We have seen the folly of bandwagons and technological panaceas. We should have learned by now about making change that persists.

Been there.

Done that.

Sadly, much of the research on making good change has been widely ignored during the current rush to network schools.

The scene that follows repeats itself all too often in places around the world as many schools have been wired and equipped without careful thought.

When schools put the cart before the horse, spending most of their money on equipment and networking rather than professional development, program devel-

"It says here you can lead a horse to water . . ."

opment, technical support and the "total cost of ownership," (van Dam, 1999), they are likely to wake up with little to show for their hefty investments.

"Not much has changed."

The superintendent and board president are wandering the halls of Millennium Elementary School with the principal. They are looking for signs that their investment in network technology has paid off.

Making Good Change

In September, each classroom was equipped with three computers tied to the district network. Millennium is a wired school.

"And you say the teachers were expecting us?" the superintendent queries, disbelief creeping into her tone.

The principal has been around long enough to recognize more than disbelief in her voice.

"I told them not to launch anything out of the ordinary. I said that you would want to see a typical Wednesday afternoon."

The superintendent stops walking and turns to face him directly.

"But, Don . . . we have walked into more than a dozen classrooms so far without seeing significant use. In two of the classrooms, we saw students doing drill and practice. In one room, we saw several students typing final drafts of papers from their handwritten work. In the other classrooms, we saw business as usual without anyone sitting near a computer. We saw no one using the Internet."

The board president, a tall woman who usually wears a broad smile is now frowning.

"Yes, Don. I have to add my own sense of disappointment. I expected to see more powerful things by now. After all, it is March. They have had the computers for seven months. Why isn't anybody using the Internet?"

Don Weatherby is not at all surprised by either woman's reaction. For more than a year he has been arguing that more is needed than wires and computers. But the district has ignored his pleas for professional development and planning resources. The focus has been

"Yessirreeee, we're wired and ready for the next century!" http://www.jerryking.com

squarely on the equipment.

He shrugs. "Well," he says, sounding proud rather than defensive, "Millennium has the best scores, the best teaching and the best community support of all the elementary schools in this district. These teachers will not do anything that might undermine that performance."

"My staff is willing to integrate technology into the program only when they see how it can help them address the state curriculum standards and improve student performance, but they are quite reluctant to use technology for technology's sake."

"Change doesn't happen in a school simply because you install new equipment," he continues, his tone quite serious now.

Don Weatherby was not sure whether his superintendent or the board president would have anything nice to say about him as they drove away from Millennium that afternoon in the superintendent's red SUV, but he was determined to go on speaking his mind.

As the district rushed to network schools and classrooms, he had often felt like the boy in the Hans Christian Andersen story who points out that the Emperor has no clothes.

Lopsided Planning Leads to Disappointments

Armed with visionary statements and promises from politicians and business folks intent on creating a "knowledge economy," we have committed a fortune to a venture severely flawed by its lopsided focus on equipment and connectivity rather than learning. What we have failed to do is demonstrate a connection between all of this new equipment and the outcomes for which schools, teachers, and principals are now rewarded (or punished.)

Evidence is accumulating from early studies that the billions of technology dollars spent each year for the past several years have had minimal impact on the daily practice of teachers across the land and scant impact on how students spend their time in schools.

Education Week's Technology Counts '99 reported that networking of schools is proceeding at a rapid pace in the States and Internet access to classrooms is much greater now than several years ago, but teacher use remains disappointing:

. . . a new **Education Week** survey has found that the typical

3

teacher still mostly dabbles in digital content, using it as an optional ingredient to the meat and potatoes of instruction.

Almost two-thirds of teachers say they rely on software or Web sites for instruction "to a minimal extent" or "not at all."

Trotter, Andrew. "Preparing Teachers For the Digital Age." **Technology Counts '99. Education Week,** September 23, 1999. http://www.edweek.org/sreports/tc99/articles/teach.htm

Sadly, funding for **Technology Counts** ceased in 1999 with dissolution of the Milken Exchange by its parent foundation.

This lack of impact should come as no surprise to those who have taken the time to learn from our past mistakes. When Sputnik caused a panic four decades back, the fear of falling behind the Russians provoked a hemorrhage of federal funds to revolutionize the ways that schools taught math, science, and just about everything.

The results of all this funding? There were many failures and some successes but a general frustration with the challenge of transferring, transporting, and transplanting changes from one system to another. Educators do have a history of trying to make change, but it is rarely read or heeded by bandwagon promoters. The consequences can be severe.

Those who cannot remember the past
are condemned to repeat it.

George Santayana

Chapter Eight of this book, "Beware the Shallow Waters: The Dangers of Ignoring the History and the Research on Change in Schools," presents a more detailed review of this literature on change,

In this introductory chapter I will briefly mention several bold stroke approaches to change that have been rarely heeded by those busily networking schools. Succeeding chapters will expand upon these strategies and others to provide the reader with a way of looking at and managing this planning process with skill and judgment.

4

Making Good Change

Basic Principles to Guide Change Efforts

1. Making good change requires a focus on a purpose likely to win broad acceptance.

Without the enthusiastic endorsement of the teachers in a building, not much change is likely to occur. To win this endorsement, the innovation being proposed must promise outcomes and benefits that match the daily realities, concerns, and desires of the staff.

Teachers have seen bandwagons come and go. They are appropriately skeptical about untested, expensive changes that seem peripheral rather than central to their purpose. They want to know how this venture will improve student performance.

In the case of educational technologies, there is often a vacuum when it comes to educational purpose. We too often network because it is "the thing to do." Teachers usually look askance at such efforts.

2. Making good change demands the cultivation and engagement of the key stakeholders within the school community, especially the classroom teachers.

The decision to network a school is usually made by powerful figures outside the school. Failure to involve building staff in the development of the learning program, the design and placement of the network resources, and a robust three to four year professional development program is courting disaster.

3. Making good change involves a strategic and balanced deployment of resources.

Schools optimize use by moving resources around to where they will do the most good. They also define resources broadly to provide a balance between the human and technical aspects of the initiative, allocating twenty-five per cent or more of their budget to professional development and a substantial salary budget to fund technical support in order to avoid the "Network Starvation" outlined in Chapter Nine.

4. Making good change necessitates time away from the "daily press" of teaching.

Fullan (1991) claims the "daily press is a major obstacle to making changes in classroom practice, as the drive to maintain forward progress often precludes an investment in sideways explorations and innovation." If districts expect to see broad-based adoption of new technologies, they must provide 30-60 hours yearly for teachers to meet, to learn, and to invent classroom units.

5. Making good change deserves a prolonged and focused commitment over three to four years.

Schools must focus their efforts on just a few worthwhile projects and maintain that focus for several years until the innovation has taken root and become routine practice for most teachers. In all too many cases, we suffer from virtual change – the appearance of change without substance and staying power.

Chapter 2 - First Things First

First things first.

Platitudes may be time worn and overly simple, but they often capture an essential truth.

First things first.

"That's obvious!" someone might grumble.

But it is startling to note how many districts fail to consider all of the key issues while neglecting, ignoring, or underfunding the essential elements of a successful technology/literacy program.

It is also surprising to watch the order in which various issues may be considered or addressed (if at all.) The metaphor of placing a cart before a horse aptly captures this failure to follow a logical sequence.

We should begin by asking what kinds of student learning we hope to promote. Those questions then logically lead to considerations of strategy and resources. Once we have a good sense of our purpose and the activities we plan to launch, we can begin to design a network that serves them well. Design should follow function.

In many cases, installation precedes discussions of purpose. Getting wired becomes the goal.

When we are planning networked schools, we should agree on a clear educational purpose. We might decide, for example, to create an "information literate school community." (McKenzie, 2000) This choice would then guide the design and development of our program.

First things first! First the purpose . . . then the design.

In all too many places, the network precedes the purpose and is distantly (if ever) related.

In all too many districts, the network is installed "cookie-cutter" fashion from school to school with little relationship to learning goals and process.

This gap between purpose and design leads to failure and waste.

First Things First

When we begin with a clearly stated purpose, we can then focus our efforts. This focus produces momentum and results. Mish mash, on the other hand, leads to confusion, scatter, and drift.

If we are constructing an information literate school community, the building blocks fall into place.

- The shape of professional development
- The nature of classroom activities
- The placement of equipment
- The layout
- The time-line
- The assessment activities

The Key Elements

A few years back I was asked to write an article about planning for technology by a leading educational journal. When I submitted the article with a list of essential elements, they cut the article in half and deleted half of the integral parts of the system. In the article, I had explained how these components must be skillfully interwoven to reinforce each other in service to improving student learning.

These elements should meld as an integrated package. Remove one component and the effort is likely to fail or flounder. Each element is as important as a keystone. Pull out the keystone and watch the arch tumble to the ground.

If we hope to see an impressive return on our investment, we cannot eliminate, short change, or underfund any of these elements.

The editors tried to pull three elements from the article . . . three of the stones from the arch I had constructed!

I pulled back my article and found a different publisher - one willing to print the article as submitted with all of the integral parts intact (see figure opposite.) The article has been extensively modified for this edition based on recent experiences with technology planning challenges as well as new planning resources now available to teachers and administrators.

1. Make learning goals and outcomes very clear

The installation of networks should support learning activities that contribute discernibly to student performance.

This challenge should be about using new tools to help students master the key concepts and skills embedded in the science, social

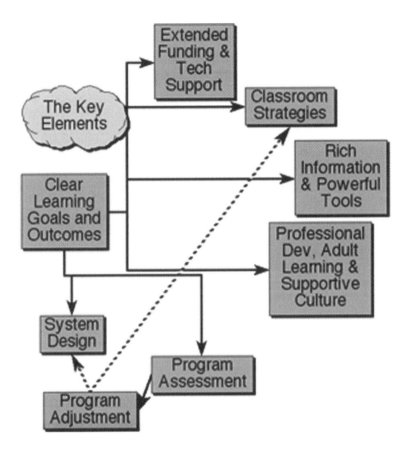

studies, art, and other curriculum standards. It is not so much about powerpointing, spreadsheeting, or word processing. The focus should be on teaching and learning strategies that actually make a difference in daily practice – on activities translating into stronger student performance. As a result of these practices and the use of these new tools, students should be able to . . .

- Read, reason and write more powerfully.
- Communicate productively with members of a global community.
- Conduct thoughtful research into the important questions, choices, and issues of their times.
- Make sense of a confusing world and a swelling tide of information.

- Perform well on the new, more demanding state tests requiring inferential reasoning, analysis, synthesis, and interpretation.

The above list reflects the high expectations of most states as they define educational purpose for this new century. A quick glance at state standards from states as diverse as California, New York, and Oklahoma show that these goals resonate from shore to shore as well as emerging from other countries.

In Western Australia, for example, the curriculum frameworks lists thirteen Overarching Learning Outcomes (see opposite page.)

Long before the design and installation of a network, a committee of educators should be asking how teachers might best develop such capabilities. In an earlier book, (McKenzie, 1993), I advocated an approach to goal setting called "Future Perfect District Technology Planning." An updated version of this approach has been included in the next chapter.

Once the goals and the outcomes are clear, the planning groups turn to the task of identifying the most promising practices and strategies to foster such growth. Most educators recognize that effective strategies are the crucial factor in shifting student patterns.

"First things first" suggests that educational purpose is clarified before strategies are selected and systems or networks are designed. The best use of new technologies is to support curriculum rich learning experiences that are standards-based and likely to elevate the skill levels of participating students.

A poem is better than a tome.

If this planning process stands any chance of modifying or enhancing the daily practice of teachers throughout the district, the committee must translate the goals into a simple but compelling format that will grab all teachers' attention and then win their support by passing various tests of practicality, worth, and reasonableness.

In all too many places, the planning documents are too long, too grand, and too imposing. They seem more like publicity documents than blueprints for change. They seem written to impress the outside community rather than inspire those responsible for implementing the changes envisioned.

Before moving forward with program and network design, it makes sense to pause for a period of reflection, consideration, and recruitment.

First Things First

First Things First

The driving question is whether or not the vast majority of teachers in the district will applaud and embrace the goals established by the committee. Drafting the document is merely an opening stage of an extended dialogue that must eventually convert skeptics and doubters into believers willing to work hard on translating goals into realities.

To skip over this recruitment and persuasion stage - as is typically the case - is somewhat like Noah pushing off from land before loading the animals.

"But why should we sail with you, Noah?"

"Because I have a great ark."

Unfortunately, promising great boats, great toys, or great bells and whistles appeals to a very small group.

We need something more substantial, more appealing, and more valuable.

And those who warn of floods, disasters, and corporate needs are also unlikely to fill their technology "arks" with eager volunteers. Even though such warnings and threats are popular strategies in some places, they show a meager understanding of schools as well as the most rudimentary truths of encouraging good change.

"The sky is falling!" wins more recruits for shelters than keyboards and literacy.

2. Identify promising learning strategies

The selection of learning strategies should follow naturally from the setting of project goals.

To illustrate the process, imagine a school that has decided to emphasize the following three outcomes previously listed (on page 11) from the **Western Australia Curriculum Frameworks**.

1. Students use language to understand, develop, and communicate ideas and information and interact with others.
3. Students recognize when and what information is needed, locate and obtain it from a range of sources and evaluate, use, and share it with others.
6. Students visualize consequences, think laterally, recognize opportunity and potential, and are prepared to test options.

Having made this choice, the next step is to identify those practices most likely to produce such outcomes. Who has done the best work on these capabilities? Which instructional or learning models have been tested until proven effective, reliable, and worth adapting for local use?

To address all three statements, the planning group surveys the field seeking models that address all three outcomes simultaneously. The group also looks for strategies capable of winning broad acceptance by the planning group.

As part of the change process, the planning team is seeking books, articles, videos and other materials that will help them to sell the learning strategies. Because they know it is a long and trying journey from theory into practice, they prefer theories and models that are firmly rooted in practical realities. They look for work that "sells itself" because it is communicated in plain but compelling terms that will appeal to classroom teachers.

The planners understand that the test of a good model involves more than good intentions. It should be appetizing, reassuring, reliable, and user friendly. With some exceptions, teachers caught in the "daily press" have little patience with models that require heroics and offer months of turbulence and trial.

"Give me something that will work on Monday morning without me sacrificing my weekend getting it all ready."

The planning group settles on the following works as a basis for addressing the three outcome statements:

1. **Mosaic of Thought: Teaching Comprehension in a Reader's Workshop.** Keene and Zimmerman (1997) offer a set of reading strategies to empower young students to read with far more understanding.
2. **Non-Fiction Matters: Reading, Writing and Research in Grades 3-8.** Harvey (1998) shows how to engage students in the exploration of serious questions with passion, resonance and coherence.
3. **Strategies that Work: Teaching Comprehension to Enhance Understanding.** Harvey and Goudvis (2000) propose a strategic approach to reading and thinking that involves questioning, visualizing, and synthesizing among others.
4. **The Art of Teaching Writing.** Calkins (1994) has little to say about technology but a great deal to say about teaching writing as process. She brings the conferencing process to life with great detail and thoroughness based on decades of working with students and teachers.
5. **Creating Writers: 6-Trait Writing Assessment and Instruction** (Spandel, 2000) and **The 6+1 Traits of Writing Center at NWREL.** (http://www.nwrel.org/eval/writing/) Spandel establishes the clear connection between revision and powerful writing.

"When we use the language of the traits, students learn that they need to examine their work for clarity of ideas, the appropriate form of organization, the alignment of purpose and audience in their voice, the precision and accuracy of their word choice, and to make sure their sentences are not only formed correctly, but also have a rhythm and cadence that makes their work read smoothly and with style."

6. **In the Middle: New Understandings about Writing, Reading, and Learning.** Atwell (1998) provides a comprehensive approach to focus student efforts on the development of understanding.

7. **Beyond Technology: Questioning, Research and the Information Literate School** (McKenzie, 2000) - Inspired by information literacy strategies being explored throughout Australia, **Beyond Technology** outlines an approach to research that makes student questioning and thinking central to schooling.

Once these models are identified, the team members must wrestle with the challenge of **orchestration**. They must figure out how to weave these program elements and possibilities into a comprehensive, coherent whole. Much like a poet, they must distill, combine and synthesize so that the pieces merge together and support each other with power, grace, and simplicity.

"And where did they teach us that skill in graduate school?"

Good question. There is little in the professional preparation of teachers or administrators that might prepare them for the development of compelling and poetic models. Sadly, it seems that much of higher education is committed to a kind of pseudo scientific approach to decision-making that often seems designed to filter out the very passions, feelings and more soulful aspects of schooling and learning that might actually ignite enthusiasm, support, and allegiance.

Fortunately, the planning team can turn to the inspirational writing and thinking of educators like Deal (1998), Lieberman (1999), Fullan (1991), and Joyce (1990) as well as other writers about organizational development like Senge (2000), Schwartz (1991), Tucker (1991) and Vail (1989).

Chapter Three - "Future Perfect Planning" - offers a brief amalgam of the best strategies of such thinkers as applied to technology planning. Translating learning models into daily practice requires a process that is somewhat analogous to seeding a cloud to create rain. The district provides the resources to enable change, but individual teachers must transform the concepts and strategies suggested by the models into actual lessons that will persist day after day.

Purgatory to start seeding clouds
Sept. 15, 2000

By Tom Sluis
Durango Herald Staff Writer
http://www.durangoherald.com/
1news3077.htm

It would make little sense to invest huge sums in these new technologies in order to win only occasional use, a special events type of implementation that involved students in doing searches and investigations a few times each year.

The goal should be to integrate the standards-based learning into every day's lessons.

The stretch from theory and model into daily practice is rarely addressed by those who bring new technologies and networks into schools, but the distance is vast. Moore (1991) writes about "Crossing the Chasm." And "chasm" may not be an exaggeration.

The challenge of moving past theory into routine practice has

Deception Pass
in Washington State

been described in great depth by Joyce and Showers. They call it the "challenge of transfer."

It is one thing to sit in the comfort of a staff development session and listen to an expert describing a new technique.

It is quite something else to make that same technique a success on Monday morning with real students in a real classroom. It is irresponsible to install networks without first equipping all teachers with the skills they need to overcome the obstacles and frustrations they will inevitably encounter when they try to use the network to deliver curriculum rich lessons.

3. Combine rich information with powerful tools in a strategic manner

Before designing a network, the planning group should begin to clarify what students will actually be doing with the new technologies. This clarification will begin with a full listing of questions worth considering such as the following:

- Which curriculum concepts, themes, and issues will students explore as part of this initiative?
- Which kinds of information sources (electronic and print) will they require to complete a thorough investigation?
- How will students sit? Alone? In pairs? In trios?
- How much time will be desired at a sitting?
- How frequently and for what duration will they need access?
- Will they need access within the social studies classroom or science classroom or further down the hall in the school library or a computer lab?
- What reference tools will they need?
- What mindware like Inspiration™ will best support and extend their thinking?
- What will the teacher be doing? How will the role of the teacher change, if at all?
- What spatial organization of the new technologies will best support the kinds of learning and teaching activities that are anticipated? Should equipment be in rows or peripheral? Would wireless notebooks work best?
- If teachers will be operating more as facilitators of learning than instructors up at the front of the room, which of the following verbs are most likely to describe their activities and what are the implications for the design of a classroom environment? of a network?

circulating	validating	moderating
redirecting	facilitating	diagnosing
disciplining	moving	troubleshooting
questioning	monitoring	observing
assessing	challenging	encouraging
guiding	motivating	suggesting
directing	watching	modeling
fascinating	seed planting	clarifying

This questioning can proceed by observing examples from other districts and by convening invention teams at each level of the district to try out various models before making a commitment..

The lessons learned and the problems avoided thanks to a year of invention and testing could save the district a huge amount of money, frustration, disappointment and embarrassment, as the focus on delivering practical lessons is likely to bring many design issues into the foreground that might not otherwise emerge until most of the infrastructure had already been nailed down.

Teaching science in a laptop classroom in Antelope Valley, California

Many school networks suffer from the "network starvation" outlined fully in Chapter Nine. To put it simply, understaffing of technical support and underfunding of information resources can lead to a network that has little of substance to offer the learners. Such networks may scream with speed and bandwidth while possessing nothing worthwhile to deliver.

When planners start with curriculum questions, it should quickly become evident that there is no "free lunch" on the Internet. No district should rely on the "free" Internet alone.

When students or teachers sit down at any desktop in the district, they should be greeted by a rich information array.

Those who have spent time exploring curriculum topics with the "free Internet" soon find that it is flawed in many respects, suffering from Info-Glut, Info-Garbage, and excessive marketing. They move swiftly to supplement the "free Internet" with other information products for which they pay a hefty price.

The goal is to equip each desktop with a dozen rich and reliable information products.

A student might select from several periodical collections, an atlas, an encyclopedia, a thesaurus, a book of quotations, a dictionary, an almanac, as well as special collections of literature, history and scientific information. The district should build a "new vertical file" for each school offering locally developed and collected data.

For those considering which information products they might purchase for their networks, there are a half a dozen or more from which to select. Because all of these are rapidly changing and improving, the choice should be based upon careful testing and evaluation in the field.

Given the cost (a site license will run several thousand dollars per school), the wise school tests these products in a lab with 30 students pushing them to their limits on actual research questions to see how well they serve the learning goals set.

Most people think of hardware when they hear the word "equipped," but a network can only support the curriculum if it is

Prominent Candidates for Purchase

- Electric Library
- EBSCO
- ProQuest Direct by UMI
- SIRS
- InfoTract
- World Book
- Encyclopedia Britannica
- Encarta
- Microsoft Bookshelf (Dictionary, Atlas, Encyclopedia, Almanac, Quotations, Thesaurus, etc.)
- Image collections & archives

Listing does not mean or imply endorsement.

loaded with information that is well organized and useful to those exploring curriculum problems and making decisions.

In addition to rich information, the planning committee should identify the most useful problem-solving applications to support student thinking - tools such as spreadsheets, databases, word processors, charting programs, outlining programs, and multimedia presentation software that will support analysis and synthesis.

Instead of spending a fortune on instructional software, the committee's emphasis upon curriculum standards inspires them to focus on tools likely to support the following activities:

- Questioning
- Planning
- Prospecting
- Collecting
- Interpreting
- Reporting
- Communicating

4. Emphasize robust professional development, adult learning, and the creation of a supportive culture

Once the program content and strategies are evident, attention should turn to mapping out the adult journey that will be required for all teachers in the district to develop the competency, the comfort, and the inclination to work effectively with the new tools.

When it comes to teachers learning and valuing the effective use of new technologies, some schools are discovering that the kinds of training programs offered in the past may not represent the most generative method of reaching a full range of teachers and their students. The key term is "generative" - meaning that behaviors and daily practice will be changed for the better as a consequence of the professional development experience.

Fortunately, some schools are now identifying approaches more likely to encourage teachers to employ these technologies on a frequent and sustained basis to enhance student learning.

Lead districts are finding that adult learning, curriculum development projects, and informal support structures are proving powerful in promoting recurrent use aimed at deep curriculum integration.

After two decades of providing software classes to teachers, we need to explore different approaches – those honoring key principles of adult learning while placing both curriculum and literacy ahead of software and technology.

Adult learning strategies are fundamentally different from training strategies and usually more promising because they are tailored to the learning styles, preferences, and needs of teachers in ways more likely to win their commitment than the approach more typical of training models.

Becker's research (1999) points to the need to do much more than teach technology skills to teachers. We must also convince them of the value of engaging students in problem-based or project-based learning with these new tools. One hundred additional hours of learning computer software is not likely to transform traditional teachers into constructivist teachers.

The transformation of teaching styles, preferences, and behaviors requires persuasion, learning by experience, and the provision of highly personalized learning journeys.

The most effective learning strategies require a change in the ways teachers spend their time and the ways they work together. Frequently we notice how informal support systems, partnerships, teams and collaborative structures may be the most efficacious elements in a broad-based change effort.

Gardening provides a useful metaphor for this process. We will see more growth if we cultivate the soil and fertilize before planting. An exclusive focus on skills and software is a bit like spreading seeds across a concrete playground.

While some maintain that reluctance to use new technologies is simply rooted in a

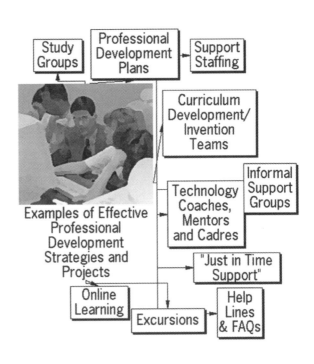

Examples of Effective Professional Development Strategies and Projects

lack of skill and confidence, there is evidence from Becker and Fullan that teachers need to be recruited. They must be convinced of the value of the new activities and then given ample time to work on teams to invent effective lessons.

In many schools, teachers are isolated from each other and preoccupied with what Fullan calls "the daily press" of getting through their schedule, focused according to Becker on state standards. Quite a few of these teachers are likely to cling to routines they have enjoyed in the past until they are equipped and encouraged to find, invent, and test new routines that are suitable and reliable replacements.

This creative exploration, invention, and testing will require a change in schools that breaks down isolation, facilitates the work of teams, and provides ample time for program development.

A previous volume, **How Teachers Learn Technology Best** (McKenzie, 1999), provides a detailed portrait of successful professional development practices.

5. Design a network system to support learning goals and activities

Once the program "horse" is directly leading the network "cart," the design process changes dramatically. The chief design issue is **utility**. The design team will want to know clearly and simply what the network can do to help produce the student learning outcomes identified as the main reason for building the network in the first place.

A. Information Power: Quality Information to the User Desktop

When a student or teacher sits down at any networked desktop, how rich and reliable are the information resources made available?

•   Does the network support student research and problem solving?
•   Does the network support powerful information harvesting in a child friendly manner?
•   Is there a periodical collection on every computer such as EBSCO, Electric Library, or ProQuest which supplies current articles on topics which are supportive of the school curriculum?
•   Is there an assortment of electronic reference tools on every computer such as an encyclopedia, an atlas, a thesaurus, and a

dictionary?

• Does the network provide user friendly access to information resources available on the Internet with appropriate "interfaces" so that teachers and students may move rapidly and efficiently to useful information?

• Does the network provide adequate bandwidth so that information arrives rapidly and efficiently?

• Does the network provide access to locally collected data (such as historical documents and water quality data) and lesson resources in support of the curriculum?

• Does the network provide access to local resources such as library books, videos, curriculum guides, board policies, personnel policies, etc.?

• Does the design of the desktop or "interface" make location of information and navigation efficient and comfortable?

B. Communication and Collaboration

Does the network reduce isolation, increase contact, and support the exchange of ideas, resources, and inventions?

• Can teachers and students conveniently store and find their work on the network so that the work builds and is always available?

• Can teachers and students exchange lessons, instructions, work, and information across the network with ease and comfort?

• Do library media specialists work with teachers to design their buildings' information menus so that they are age-appropriate, coherent, and curriculum relevant?

• Can teachers and students exchange information and ideas with teachers, students, experts, and others regionally or globally?

• Can teachers and other staff members share good ideas, questions, interests, and needs through e-mail exchanges?

• Can the administrative staff communicate important information and expectations through the network to all groups that have a need to know the information?

C. Access

Does the network offer frequent, easy, and convenient access to resources so that the rich information and powerful tools become part of the daily life of the schools as well as all the staff members and students?

• If all students wished to make use of computers on a daily basis, how many minutes would be possible? If they wish to spend three or four hours in a week writing an essay or doing research, is that possible?

• Does the amount of access match program needs?

• To what extent are computers located so that students and staff may use them when they need them?

• Can computers be moved around conveniently to support learning goals in a flexible manner?

• Are all computers located where they are likely to be used 85% or more of the time?

• Are computers placed in specific locations because they are needed there for predefined purposes and goals or are they placed in locations without any clear purpose other than balanced distribution?

• Are computers distributed in line with learning models and research that have been proven effective or are they placed in locations without any clear purpose other than balanced distribution?

• Is there an appropriate balance between "open access" computers as opposed to computers located in scheduled access rooms and labs where an "appointment" is required?

• Is there a plan to move away from "lab-centered" access to "distributed" access as staff and students develop the skills and capacity to sustain a "distributed" system?

• Is there a clear understanding of "critical mass" - the minimal essential number of classroom computers required to sustain significant use? Self-contained elementary classrooms require one computer for every 4-5 students. Secondary classrooms require one computer for every 2-3 students but most secondary teachers prefer access to such resources only 20-25 per cent of the time because coverage pressures make anything more quite unlikely.

D. Evidence of Use

Can we be sure the technology is used frequently in ways which support our goals?

• Is there a system to keep track of utilization trends and rates in each building?

• Is there a clearly stated expectation about utilization rates?

• Is there a planning mechanism to keep utilization "on the table?"

• What happens if utilization falls below expectations?
• Are all staff expected to do "their fair share?" How are these expectations expressed and then monitored?
• Are the expectations written into curriculum documents as required learning experiences?

Tilting toward Utility

Without a strong curriculum focus, network design criteria will tend to center around the following criteria and issues:

• **Efficiency** - How well does data flow across the network?
• **Speed** - How quickly does the network handle the data tasks assigned to it?
• **Reliability** - Can users count on the network to be operating without interruption?
• **Security** - Are data transmissions safe from outside intrusions and interference?
• **Cost** - Does the network operate within a reasonable budget?
• **Low Maintenance** - Does the network perform its tasks without requiring frequent technical support interventions?
• **Transparency** - Does the network operate in the background without requiring user awareness of network functions and protocols?

Unfortunately, a focus on these utilitarian issues can seriously damage the prospects for curriculum rich use of networks, as the design may be shifted away from what actually works for teachers. The very features that are most important to teachers . . . flexibility, portability, frequent use, and relatively open, user-friendly systems can seem threatening to network supervisors who might see heavy traffic and open access threatening to undermine performance and stability.

Even though it seems apparent that networks should serve teachers, students, and learning, in many cases networks become self-serving in the sense that their health and functioning becomes a goal separate and above the whole issue of student learning and curriculum.

Does the network hum? Does it scream?

6. Provide extended funding, technical support, and commitment

Because few districts understand the full cost of owning and operating a robust network, there is a tendency to provide insufficient technical support staff and insufficient funding for network development over time. While the computer vendors and network software companies have excelled at the art of promoting rapid obsolescence under the guise of "enhancement" and "upgrades," districts rarely develop an equipment replacement schedule that accurately reflects the reality of keeping up with those enhancements.

Without a comprehensive and all inclusive, long term budget to keep them vibrant, networks have a tendency to "rust." This means rather simply that performance can suffer as new software will start to drag down the speed and response of desktop units bought for an earlier stage of development.

Without appropriate levels of technical support, a district is likely to suffer from what I have called "network starvation" (Chapter Nine). In addition to diminished network reliability and efficiency, such districts also tend to experience a lack of network resource development to support curriculum goals because there are too few technicians to install and maintain the information products required for a robust experience. Even worse, the lack of technical staff can foster a climate of tight control over network resources that may block teachers and librarians from shaping the network experience at a building level. In many districts, educators are not allowed access to file servers and web sites, so they are unable to influence the design of resources in a learner friendly manner.

7. Match rigorous program assessment to learning goals and student outcomes

The recent networking of schools has been accomplished with remarkably little attention to the assessment of results. The lack of data gathering is akin to sailing blindly through the fog. Because we are exploring many uncharted seas, the risks of shipwreck and failure are quite high. And those risks are made all the more serious by a failure to climb the mast so that the program can be adjusted in response to data gathered as the innovation proceeds.

In the best implementations, we combine our knowledge of best practice in other districts with intense local data gathering to find out which strategies are working and which ones are failing or disappointing. Denial flourishes in a system without assessment, and the program can lunge forward toward shallows and hazards without anyone recognizing that there are problems until it may be too late.

The reason we gather data is to steer the program past obstructions and hazards toward success. We shed failing strategies. We redouble commitment to strategies that are working. We gradually shift our energies to those activities that produce the best results.

Without data, all strategies appear equal. We rob both teachers and students of opportunity. We fail to make the most of our resources. We fall more deeply into the trap of doing technology for technology's sake.

Without evidence of student learning, districts can hide behind measures of success that have little to do with schooling.

How many computers? How many wired classrooms? How deep is the penetration?

This preoccupation with counting equipment and measuring penetration is characteristic of industry funded reports like the Star Chart (1999) that make a fantastic leap from the possession of equipment to assumptions of program quality.

8. Monitor and adjust program elements and strategies in response to experience

In line with the assessment outlined above, each school will need a committee to adjust the program as more is learned about what is working and what is not. Tempting though it is to walk away from this challenge once network installation is complete, the installation is merely a prelude to program development.

Perhaps because of wildly exaggerated promises and forecasts of benefits likely to emerge thanks to networking, many schools fail to install the human decision-making apparatus that is required to convert this investment in networking from what some might call "Fool's Gold" (2000) into something of real value. Without ongoing leadership and program development, it is unlikely that the network will make much of an impact upon student learning.

Chapter 3 - Future Perfect Planning

Nuts, bolts, and wire closets have a way of obscuring the big picture, the dream and what former President George Bush once called "the vision thing."

Note: In some respects, this chapter should precede the one before it, but for many districts, the aspirations of this chapter may exceed the local tolerance for delay as many seek to network rapidly. For some this chapter will be supplemental. For others it will seem fundamental.

As mentioned earlier, plans may go awry as some schools proceed with networking. In many cases, techno-enthusiasts and planners lose sight of the learning possible if networks are created with a focus on ways that students communicate, gather information, and reason about the most important questions in life.

Sadly, a preoccupation with the practical details of connecting all classrooms to the Internet may elevate **connectivity** to prime goal status - displacing **learning** from the top of the list. But, despite claims to the contrary, connectivity is not especially new to schools and offers little of note by itself. Classrooms have been connected to television networks for decades, for example, without achieving the miracles their proponents predicted.

This chapter explores an approach to planning that might help protect schools from such a narrow focus on the nuts and bolts of networking. Adapted from the corporate world to support planning in the educational world, **Future Perfect Planning** is an approach to the future that elevates our thinking to focus upon the most important issues.

Future Perfect?

Future Perfect Planning (FPP) is based upon the work of Stan Davis (1997). Davis offers **FPP** as an alternative to strategic planning, which he criticizes as being too wedded to past habits and mind-sets.

Davis sees **FPP** as a powerful way to connect one's greatest aspirations with the business of constructing high quality futures. If an organization hopes to emphasize its highest aspirations, **FPP** is an approach that lifts attention from limiting factors and obstacles to possibilities.

Because strategic planning relies heavily upon the projection of trends, Davis argues, it is ill prepared to help us with innovation and often hinders significant change. Strategic planning does not anticipate or prepare us well for "discontinuous change" like the breakup of the USSR or the arrival of e-commerce or the privatization of education.

Unfortunately, many school districts, eager to follow corporate examples pushed on educators during the "restructuring" days of the 1980s and 1990s, have adopted the strategic planning models that Davis criticizes, models that may have left major corporations like IBM, AT&T, Firestone, and Microsoft unprepared to cope with major changes in their business environments.

For quite some time now, it has been fashionable for some corporations to suggest that schools act and plan like they do, even though we have plenty of evidence that schools change, grow and thrive in ways that are profoundly different from the experience of corporations. We also have plenty of evidence that their planning models may fail some of these corporations.

Instead of asking what benefits new technologies can bring to students and classrooms, many districts have bypassed that question entirely, jumping immediately to "How do we network?" They leap prematurely to installation and implementation issues.

FPP devotes far more time and energy to possibilities and outcomes. It is a fundamentally optimistic and hopeful approach to planning futures. It reaches further into the future, casts off more preconceptions, challenges conventional wisdom, explores new territory, and calls up dreams that have all too often been suppressed, discouraged or frowned upon.

> *This is not just a matter of doing yesterday's work a little bit better.*

Wisely installed, supported and implemented, new technologies might sustain substantially better learning systems - experiences that would extend beyond the assumptions and the boundaries of older school practices.

Under the best circumstances, networks and wireless laptops might improve the way students and teachers form questions, explore their worlds and build answers. But these same tools, installed with the wrong strategies, might instead contribute little of note.

The challenge is to unleash the full potential of new technologies to support student learning unhampered by what we might call "smokestack" conceptions better suited to a factory-based economy. **FPP**, to be described in the next few sections, empowers a district to view the future with imagination and an open mind.

In **The Social Life of Information** (2000) Brown and Duguid warn us about corporate "infoenthusiasts."

Brown and Duguid are insiders. They spend their lives where information technologies do their best and their worst. Fully acquainted with the hype and promises of information cheerleaders, Brown and Duguid warn that ". . . it can be easy for a logic of information to push aside the more practical logic of humanity." (p. 18)

They fear that an obsession with information can lead to a kind of tunnel vision with planners ignoring much of what lies within the periphery.

Note: John Seely Brown is the Chief Scientist at Xerox Corporation and Director of the Xerox PaloAlto Research Center (PARC) and Paul Duguid is a research specialist in Social and Cultural Studies in Education at the University of California at Berkeley.

When I first wrote about **Future PerfectPlanning** in 1993, the notion of placing networked computers in every classroom remained a pipe dream for most schools.

At that time, the Internet was mostly text based and not very inspiring. It took a vivid imagination to consider the possibilities. And most folks were too busy with local area networks to think about wide area networks and global networks.

As this book goes to press in 2001, we find ourselves busily networking schools and laying cables just as **wireless** becomes a practical choice. Much planning for technology is now dominated by trends and marketing pressures. First a district installs equipment without adequate professional development or technical support and then it lurches in the opposite direction, over correcting the course like a drunken sailor.

Planning good change is not about jumping from gimmick to

gizmo. It is not about leaping onto every bandwagon zooming across the educational landscape.

Planning good change requires a more thoughtful approach with greater vision.

Because **Future Perfect Planning** is especially well suited to thinking about innovation, this book provides a brief introduction to its techniques and promises.

Step One - The Creation of a Planning Team

As outlined in the previous chapter, before thoughtful decisions can be made about which technologies to purchase and how to use them, the district or school must clarify its learning priorities and preferences. An educational planning team comprised of teachers, students, administrators, community members and board members should spend a year or more clarifying the mission of the district in simple but compelling terms.

The composition of this planning team should be mixed and representative of the many different perspectives, styles and aspirations held by each of the prime groups.

It is far too easy to load the planning group with the technoenthusiasts and infoenthusiasts Brown and Duguid (2000) warn us about in their book. If a district falls into the trap of overloading the committee with zealots, the planning process may distort the agenda.

Surprisingly, a committee comprised of skeptics as well as enthusiasts may find a healthier pathway, one that addresses the needs and interests of all the participants rather than a select group.

If one of the goals of this process is an implementation that wins and deserves broad based support and participation, then the selection of committee members is a crucial step in the process of gaining that support. There are several qualities worth emphasizing while selecting members:

1. **Positive Spirit** - It is important that all members of the group be capable of dreaming, believing, trusting, and exploring. Informed and constructive skepticism is perfectly fine. Naysaying becomes a big drag on the process.
2. **Open Mindedness** - Exploration of new terrain requires participants to think the unthinkable and consider new prospects with an open and willing mind. Those who know all the answers rarely find the new ones.
3. **Empathy** - In order to create a plan with broad-based support, the

members of this group must be good at understanding the needs, interests, and feelings of all the key players - students, teachers, parents, etc. The capacity to sit in someone else's seat and see things the way they do becomes a major element in the success of the committee's work.

4. **Curiosity** - As the committee must focus upon the unknown, the unfamiliar and the uncharted potentials of new ways of learning, members should feel thrilled and eager about the discovery process. This search will require a thirst for new knowledge and understanding, a willingness to step out of the comfort zone into new terrain.

5. **Impartiality** - It works best when no members have entangling relationships and conflicts of interest that might blind the person to exciting possibilities or lead to turf related conflicts as the partisan for one desktop or corporation goes to war against those representing others.

6. **Inventiveness** - Because the planning process is about finding new pathways and new approaches, participants should be skilled at looking at challenges from a variety of angles through a variety of lenses in order to identify the most promising combinations and variations. They should be able to think this way both individually and as a group member, listening, understanding, melding, and creating as a team member whose best ideas are provoked by the thinking of the team.

Step Two - What do we care about?

Future perfect planning is rooted in dreams and aspirations. Instead of plodding along heavily yoked by the disappointments and harsh realities of "life in the trenches," the planners sincerely consider the prospects of transforming classrooms into something far better.

- Can we spark the curiosity of more children?
- Can we equip a larger percentage of students with great reading, writing, and thinking skills?
- Can we broaden students' perspectives so they acquire a global view?
- Can we inspire a deeper and more thoughtful approach to important questions and issues?
- Can we create a generation of students who are not only skilled and eager but full of confidence?

Each planning group begins its work by identifying shared aspirations and values. This process often requires a succession of group experiences such as workplace visits, common readings and the viewing of dramatic films and videos likely to stimulate thinking about a changing world.

This stage is somewhat like the seeding of clouds to create rain or snow. The group begins with stimulating experiences but moves toward consensus.

What do we care about?

Step Three - Where are we now?

The committee will assess the district's current level of planning for technologies by completing the **District Technology Assessment Form** in **Appendix A**. The assessment form will help to identify categories of planning and thinking often overlooked by districts as they install new technologies and networks.

Step Four - Development of scenarios

An important difference between **FPP** and strategic planning is the perspective from which each views the future. Strategic planners stand in the present looking ahead toward the year 2010 asking how present trends may twist and turn during this decade.

FPP places us in the year 2010 and asks us to imagine what learning might be like for a 7 year-old or a 14 year-old. FPP encourages us to taste, smell, and see learning as the child might, free of any barriers or restrictions. After months of creating, swapping, and clarifying such images of educational futures, the planning group moves toward shared scenarios, two or three prime stories that contain the most important aspirations held by members of the group.

Schwartz offers a five step guide to the building of scenarios that may serve with Davis' book as key resources to guide the planning process. He explains that scenarios are stories to help us break past our mind-sets to see futures which might otherwise be blocked from sight. As far back as 1981, prior to Glasnost, he and fellow scenario-builders at Shell Oil foresaw the breakup of the USSR using such techniques.

Appendix B provides an example of a brief educational scenario describing two young girls using a hand held computing device (PDA) with voice recognition to tackle a challenging social studies research task.

Future Perfect Planning

According to Schwartz, the planning group should pass through each of the following phases:

1. Articulating the Mind Set

What are the key values and belief systems that have tended to dictate school behaviors in the past? They are often submerged and hidden from view. Schwartz urges us to uncover and then examine them to see if they are still valid.

For example, it may be the prevailing sense of teachers that they should dictate most of the learning that takes place in classrooms while students follow their leads. Under Becker's categories of teaching styles, this approach might be called "traditional." If the prevailing beliefs and practices within a district are tilted toward teacher control rather than student exploration, this "mind set" will have a very strong influence upon how new technologies might be used, if at all.

Without a substantial investment in transformative professional development and adult learning to persuade teachers to shift toward more project-based approaches, any committee aspirations for schooling with an emphasis upon information literacy would prove far fetched.

This process of identifying operating beliefs helps to set up the planning dialectic of contrasting **what is** to **what should be**. It is not enough for a committee to proclaim desirable ends. If the existing mind sets go unexamined and unidentified, they are likely to shape the future in many powerful ways conflicting with the committee's best hopes.

The change process in schools usually requires substantial investment in persuasion as well as learning. The persuasion cannot begin until existing attitudes are well known and evident.

2. Information Hunting and Gathering

The planning committee seeks models to emulate. Rather than reinventing the wheel from scratch, they look for those school districts and schools that have successfully implemented programs and goals similar to their own.

Sadly, there are not many outstanding models to emulate when it comes to curriculum rich implementation that is well supported with professional development reaching all staff members.

The committee may attend many workshop sessions and visit many schools that prove disappointing as marketing hype and reputation often exceed classroom realities. Many of these programs thrive thanks to the special efforts of pioneers and early adopters while late adopters and skeptics maintain business as usual.

Future Perfect Planning

Just as early immigrants to America were promised streets paved with gold, many districts are swayed by promises of golden rewards in the form of student achievement and performance that are rarely substantiated with credible data.

This lack of models means that the committee will have to look further afield and must exercise more creative thinking to identify change strategies and program elements that will actually shift how students learn, think and grow. They will also need to consider the very large challenge of convincing teachers that these shifts are worthwhile, for without the enthusiastic endorsement and participation of the vast majority of the staff, little change can happen.

It is all too fashionable to pursue a strategy of evangelism, heaping special opportunities on a vanguard of techno-enthusiasts to lead the way for all the others, but this strategy can often backfire and lead to anger and resentment.

In trying to build understanding, Schwartz claims that many organizations are blind-sided by their tendency to gather data selectively - data that serves to confirm old mind-sets, behaviors and visions. Data that might force a reconsideration is often screened away, according to Schwartz, and so he recommends intentionally wandering far afield to collect information that might alert the group to the driving forces and uncertainties mentioned next.

Because schools have traditionally ignored workplace realities, for example, the committee must venture out to see how technologies are transforming the ways problems are solved and information is handled. The goal is to look closely at the present while considering developments and shifts likely to arrive in the near and far term.

This visit strategy is more fully explained in **How Teachers Learn Technology Best** (1999) but a section is included in this chapter to illustrate the kinds of questions that deserve attention.

The committee identifies a dozen or more organizations that have embraced the new technologies with some style, enthusiasm, and success. Ideally, the list of organizations should include a good number of not-for-profit groups such as museums, libraries, hospitals, and government agencies. But these should be balanced with a rich variety of profit making companies such as banks, manufacturing outfits, architectural firms, entertainment complexes, and shipping companies.

The committee is split up into teams of four to five members, each to visit one work place.

When these planning teams visit, members will act as anthropologists and sociologists. They will conduct research . . . trying to understand how life is changing and how they can best prepare students for

Future Perfect Planning

Questions for Workplace Visits

Effectiveness

Process - In what ways do information technologies (**IT**) contribute to an effective flow of work and production?

Product - In what ways does **IT** improve the quality of products or services?

Customization - How does **IT** make service relevant to client needs, interests and desires?

Teaming

Concern - Does **IT** make this organization more or less caring, warm, and humane?

Culture - What changes in beliefs, attitudes and behaviors result from an increasingly technological workplace?

Adult Learning - How does this organization support the continuous growth of employees?

Competencies - What capacities are important? What thinking, communicating, persuading, and information skills?

Traits - What personal qualities and traits - such as curiosity, ingenuity, empathy, originality, and persistence - are desirable and prized?

Planning

Future View - How does this organization keep an eye on the horizon and prepare for changing technologies? What are the most important changes you see arriving in the next twelve months? Two years? Five years? Ten years?

Responsibility - Who is responsible for planning and thinking about the future? How are their efforts synchronized with other functions? How do they try to engage all stakeholders in such thinking? To what extent are they successful?

such changes. For this reason, the questioning process is paramount.

A sample list of questions is offered on page 35.

The day begins with an introductory session for all teams to acquaint them with the schedule, the purpose of the day and a suggested list of questions. Each team is then encouraged to expand and adapt this list of questions before heading off to conduct their inquiries.

The first half of the day is devoted to visits. During the second half, the teams gather to share their findings and discuss the implications of their discoveries. The committee draws from the visits a list of trends and driving forces to help inform the goal setting and deliberations that will form the basis for a mission statement.

3. Identifying and Exploring the Driving Forces

Driving forces differ dramatically from trends because they are often hidden from view, creating a stir of some kind not easily tied back to the original cause. A decade back, major driving forces such as choice, life-style, discounting, and value-adding were prominent, but now a planning committee will want to explore the implications of globalization, e-commerce, shifting demographics, and what some commentators call the "digital economy" or "knowledge economy" - keeping in mind the reality that many commentators are promoters and cheerleaders.

A careful examination of claims made for the new dot.com future should include a healthy dose of skepticism. The planning committee's awareness of such driving forces will be instrumental in laying the groundwork for thinking about possible and likely futures.

4. Uncovering Predetermined Elements and Critical Uncertainties

Some factors, such as demographic trends bringing an increasingly mixed population, are essentially predetermined and highly predictable. In the case of education, the source of funding would be an example of critical uncertainty, as school finance suits in many states turn the funding rules upside down and many national leaders push for school choice and the use of vouchers. The possibility of schools operating on a free-market basis with parental choice is a very real critical uncertainty. With the growth of online learning opportunities, the whole issue of locus - where learning will occur - becomes less of a given. This is both a risk and an opportunity for schools as they can take advantage of new delivery systems to alter the shape and nature of the school day, possibly even freeing teachers of some of the custodial aspects of schools to spend more time on professional and program development.

5. Composing a Plot

Having passed through the previous stages, the planning group begins the story writing. It often pays, according to Schwartz, to build three scenarios, one optimistic, one pessimistic and one in the middle.

Once dozens of scenarios are completed, the planning team should proceed through the phases listed by Schwartz and move toward creation of the two or three prime scenarios mentioned earlier. The collection of scenarios should embrace the major themes that are most important to members of the group.

Step Five - Creation of an educational mission statement

In order to guide the decision-making and strategies of school planners, whether it be with regard to technology, curriculum or staff development, the planning team must translate its scenarios into a few brief sentences that will shape choices.

Mission statements should not be confused with board of education philosophies, which usually attempt to cover all possible goals. Mission statements focus upon a few key goals that will receive special attention. They should also clarify some process issues.

An example follows:

> The Mission ISD will help students to become well-informed, imaginative, and thoughtful decision-makers. Our students will be capable of working independently or collaboratively to create workable solutions to complex problems. We will encourage them to act in a caring, compassionate, and empathic manner. Toward those ends, we will stress activities that challenge students to do their own thinking and learning.

Each district should form its own statement tied to the priorities and views of the planning group and the board of education. This statement should then work to help other, newly constituted planning groups to sift through the options and possibilities that lie ahead.

Future Perfect Planning

Step Six - Using the mission statement for technology planning

As the process moves from goal setting to action planning, the committee might well use the metaphor of building a cathedral to help guide its thinking and planning. No cathedral stands much chance of withstanding the attacks of time and nature without solid foundations and flying buttresses, and yet the real beauty of the structure might lie in the spires stretching to the sky, in the stained glass windows capturing wondrous images, or in the services and music contained within the structure. It is much the same with technologies and learning.

Effective programs require human and technical infrastructures somewhat like a cathedral's foundations and flying buttresses.

As infotects, much like the master builders and architects of old, planners should be asking which elements of the foundation are most likely to withstand the tests of time, avoiding shortcuts, and false economies. They must seek infrastructure that is balanced, flexible, powerful, adaptable, and expandable.

Planners must avoid the creation of thick, highly detailed planning and curriculum documents that might block learning, experimentation, and innovation. Brevity and clarity are paramount.

I T (Information Technology) does not transform schools (by ITself.)

It is time we replace the term "Information Technology" with "Information Literacy." **IT** is mainly about flow - the movement of information through networks of various kinds. But information in a time of info-glut and data smog (Shenk, 1998) can actually interfere with learning and understanding.

Information abundance can overwhelm and drown the learner in irrelevant and unreliable information. **IL** (Information Literacy) is mainly about developing understanding and insight. Literacy is about interpretation of information to guide decisions, solve problems, and steer through uncertain, complex futures.

What we need most now is a commitment to Information Literacy by schools as they strive to improve the reading, writing, and thinking of their students. This will entail a sincere and robust investment in professional development to help this generation of teachers learn how to use the new electronic tools in ways that count.

Problems of Readiness and Preparation

Market Data Retrieval (1999) claims that more than 60% of the teachers replying to a survey indicated that they were not well prepared to use these technologies in their classrooms.

"Building the Digital Curriculum," **Education Week, Technology Counts '99**, makes it clear that we have much work to do before we see widespread integration.

We are witnessing an equipment shopping spree that violates good sense and ignores what we know about changing schools. Schools have become the target for an unprecedented technology binge that is some times more about decoration and status rather than achievement.

Early adopting states are now (belatedly) commissioning "audits" that do little to demonstrate any return on investment. Changing classrooms from "sage on the stage" traditional models to include "guide on the side" student-centered strategies and activities requires a prolonged commitment to professional development - one that is well beyond the resources and the savvy of most school districts.

We have few models to emulate and little evidence that this transformation of teaching styles is even possible. Adding to that issue is a widespread failure to move computers about strategically in order to optimize benefits. In far too many cases, computers are spread thinly across classrooms without regard for readiness and with too little "cultivation" of the classrooms or their occupants.

Problems of Philosophy and Inclination

Hank Becker's research shows that "traditional" teachers are three times less likely to allow students to use new technologies than "constructivist" teachers. Many teachers are inclined to stick with traditional teaching.

We apparently suffer from poor preparation as well as a lack of inclination. While many "traditional" teachers in Becker's study express some desire to spend more time on student-centered learning, they complain that new state curriculum standards and tests leave them little time or room to support such activities.

Inclination is rarely addressed as a technology challenge. Sadly, there is little written about the reluctant, late adopting, traditional teachers and

http://fno.org   http://www.jerryking.com

"This Internet is great for research. I think my report on California breaks a Guinness World Record. 174.513 separate sources!"

how to enlist their support in the effort.

This failure helps to explain their lack of use.

Chapter 5 - The New New Thing

New is not necessarily better, but these days the new new thing usually sells well. Note: **The New New Thing : A Silicon Valley Story** by Michael Lewis (2000)

We have a new test of time.

- Is it hip?
- Is it fashionable?
- Is it e-commerce? e-schooling?
- Wired?
- Digital?

Sometimes it seems as if the educational world is rocked by the revolutionary shifts taking place in the business world.   Stones cast into corporate ponds create ripples and tidal waves that all too often crash on our educational shores. "If it isn't online, just how good could it be?" is too often the question these days. What ever happened to value?

The stock market has been torn between the "old economy" and the "new economy." On March 28, 2000, **U.S.A. Today** announced that Cisco Systems "bypassed" Microsoft as the world's most valuable company - based on stock price - as Microsoft stock fell some 40 billion dollars in one day in anticipation of unfavorable court rulings. Cisco Systems was trading at 136 times "what the company was expected to earn." Its business? Providing an array of products to support the networking of the digital economy.

On Friday, April 14, 2000, the stock market fell the most points in history.

What we had in 1999-2000 was a bubble - an investment frenzy that persisted for several years and made fortunes for many investors.

The dot.com bubble was closely associated with the **Emperor's New Clothes**. Those who study history will recall that periods of rampant speculation are usually followed by busts - periods of readjustment to reality. As this book goes to press, commentators jokingly refer to **dot.compost.**

When financial bubbles burst, sometimes the consequences are felt in very human ways, as we all recall photographs of men lined up at Depression soup kitchens.

But what happens when educational bubbles burst?

Financial Bubbles of the Past

The South Seas Bubble	1711-1720
The Mississippi Scheme	1717-1720
Panic of 1819 (USA)	1819
Panic of 1837 (USA)	1837
California Gold Rush	1848-1849
Panic of 1857 (USA)	1857
Panic of 1893 (USA)	1893
Black Friday	Sept. 24, 1869
The Klondike, Canada	1897-1898
Panic of 1907 (USA)	1907
The Great Depression	1929

Educational Bubbles of the Past

Open Classrooms
The New Math
The New Social Studies
Instructional TV
ITIP - Madeline Hunter

To what extent are schools vulnerable to this bubble phenomenon?

Bandwagons and Trainwrecks

We have seen thirty or more educational reform initiatives sweep through schools during the past three decades. Open classrooms. Instructional TV. Programmed learning. The principal as instructional leader. Cooperative Learning. Madeline Hunter's ITIP. LOGO. Effective Schools.

Some of these have been exciting and enjoyable. Most have promised great change. Many have delivered less than they promised.

The New New Thing

Traits of a Robust Bandwagon

- Exorbitant fanfare and marketing efforts
- Emphasis upon testimonials
- Lack of credible data
- Face validity
- Lighthouse appeal (and price)
- Distortion of priorities and budgets

Sometimes it seems as if schools specialize in virtual change as fads create sparks, spinning wheels, and the appearance of change without actually making much difference in daily practice. Walls come down. Walls reappear. We restructure, realign, reform and introduce Total Quality Management while life in Mrs. Jacob's classroom goes on much as it did 30 years ago.

Changing schools is good for business. Walk through the exhibits of any major conference and take in the vast menu of options available to transform schools. The products, the promises, and the promotions rise like a mountain range. But take a look at the storage rooms and closets of many schools where well intended innovations and products often spend their final days. Can we afford to spend billions on unproven change strategies without a plan that emphasizes literacy and student results?

In recent times, networking schools has risen to the top of the list of initiatives, as schools have wired and cabled so that all classrooms can feast on the Internet. Unfortunately, the wiring of schools has proceeded without respecting what we have learned about making real change in schools.

The Laptop Promise (and Fallacy)

According to some promoters, if you buy a laptop for each student, you are likely to win the following benefits:

- Better writing
- Expanded knowledge
- Increased achievement - higher scores
- Improved skills for the modern workplace
- Enhanced learning and teaching efficiency
- Heightened motivation for all involved
- Enriched preparation for global citizenry

43

- Elevated problem-solving and decision-making
- Intensified student-centered learning
- Augmented teaming and cooperation

Most teachers know that buying laptops for students without investing heavily in professional development and program development is unlikely to improve student performance, but the sales pitch rolls onward.

So far, this marketing ploy has worked most effectively with parents of independent school students who can be persuaded that today's investment in a laptop is a path to a dot.com future paved with stock options and lucrative benefits. Extravagant claims tied to Net Generation potentials create a brisk business for the vendors, but what about the faculty and its legitimate skepticism about these digital tools?

Many independent school teachers take pride in a studied classicism. They know that the interpretation of a Shakespearean sonnet requires earnest concentration on meaning without much intervention by machines - smart or otherwise. They are not easily convinced that a laptop will do much to ease that translation process.

A few years into the laptop miracle, severe questions may surface.

The initial rush of excitement sparked by the arrival of the laptops may fade as some teachers ignore the new tools while pursuing the time-tested teaching strategies that have served them well for decades.

Students keep track of the times they are asked to use the laptops. A few days go by without use. The laptop seems heavy.

"Why not leave the laptop home? Will anyone notice? Anyone care?"

A week goes by.

Nobody notices.

Mrs. Rinaldo asks the class to use their laptops to begin an essay but only nine of the seventeen students have brought their laptops to school.

Without robust program and professional development, laptop programs are unlikely to make much of a difference.

Resisting Seductive Bandwagons

Without surrendering to old-fashioned, close-minded notions of schooling, teachers and school leaders can team to resist fashion, trend, fad and the latest rage while embracing promising practices and opportunities. Basic principles should guide the planning process and act as filters to fend off the least valuable experiments and ventures.

- Does this new approach improve the quality of student thought?
- How much value and substance is evident?
- What data is available to demonstrate results?
- Can we expect a reasonable return on investment?

It is not so important that our school be early in the adoption of a new thing. What matters is whether or not the adoption is managed well and the outcomes prove worthwhile.

"We've lost a lot less books
since we brought in the
INTERNET."

Chapter 6 - Beware the Wizard

"It is better to fail in originality than to succeed in imitation."

Herman Melville

Samantha Peters is sitting in the staff lounge correcting student PowerPoint™ presentations on her laptop while chatting with several other teachers who are correcting papers from their classes.

"How are they coming out?" asks her friend, Terri, a member of her department who has been reluctant to engage her students in the creation of multimedia reports.

"I hate to admit it, Terri, but I am seeing too much flash and not enough thought. I am getting the same few clip art images over and over again. Lots of special effects but not much rigor."

Terri suppresses a triumphant "I told you so," and smiles compassionately.

At this point a third teacher chimes in . . . "I think there is a solution," she says.

Samantha and Terri look over in surprise. Helen Brown is a veteran. No one knows exactly how old she is, but she has outlasted every other teacher and principal who ever worked in this high school, and she is known for her rigor and her high standards. She is not generally thought of as a technology enthusiast.

"I had the same disappointing results when I started," she continues, "but I changed the way I assigned the reports to give students clear expectations. I warned them against the use of wizards, templates and clip art. Told them I'd mark them down if they painted by numbers." Explained how I would reward originality and penalize them for sliding by with formulaic creations."

Samantha is curious now. "You used the word 'formulaic' with them?"

"Sure I did. We spent an entire class looking at standardization as a market trend . . . the rise of fast food restaurants, Big Macs, and what some people have alternately called the disneyfication or GAPping of America."

"We looked at templates for resumes and questioned how they might hinder or help a job search."

"And they got the message?" Terri asks.

"Certainly did. And then I had them look over some assessment rubrics that really drove the point home. Their presentations were vastly different from those submitted in the previous semester."

Samantha and Terri exchange looks. They are impressed and not a little surprised.

"And where did you find this strategy?" asks Terri.

Helen Brown shrugged. "Most of it was classic. I've been waging a battle against glib thinking for decades."

Teachers in some networked schools are beginning to complain about a new brand of plagiarism and a shift of student work toward the glitzy and the glib.

Along with the facility of new technologies comes the danger of facile, superficial thinking and the uncritical use of the slim "library" of templates and images accompanying a scanty number of software programs. Some students are handing in reports that are marvels of cut-and-paste thinking decorated with special effects and visual knick-knacks that belong in a young child's rubber stamp set.

In our zeal to make powerful use of new technologies in schools, we have sometimes forgotten the classic strategies used by effective teachers for decades to show students the difference between quality work and imitative work. We have sometimes been too quick to embrace and install electronic products that offer gimmicks, wizards, clip art, and templates that seem innocent (and neutral) enough when adopted but subtly work to undermine the communicative power of our students.

Fortunately, there are ways to teach students to be critical consumers of wizards, clip art, and templates. More importantly, there are strategies to teach our students to be their own wizards and magicians, to shrug off the commercially available gimmicks in favor of their own magic. With the right approach, we can make them proud of their originality and fresh thinking. This chapter offers a half dozen ways to raise a generation of students to use what Harry Potter and his friends might call "good magic."

1. Valuing Originality

We begin as the teacher in the scenario with clear purpose. All students from early elementary to secondary are introduced to the difference between standardization on the one hand and originality on the other. The school takes a stand. Formulaic and imitative work is strongly discouraged. It is not even graded. It is returned for re-working. Students know that imitation is not an option. More importantly, they spend time exploring these issues as they influence the quality of life.

"When (if ever) is a standard hamburger desirable?"
"When (if ever) is a customized hamburger important?"
"When (if ever) is a standard resume desirable?"
"When (if ever) is a customized resume desirable?"

2. Clarifying Standards

We adopt and communicate clear standards to govern the assessment of student presentations, reports and performances. Students know at the outset of a project which traits and qualities are essential.

As an example, we provide clear rubrics for valued behaviors so that students may take a hand at self-assessment.

We may use the Multimedia Rubrics available from ISTE.
http://www2.ncsu.edu/ncsu/cep/midlink/rub.multi.htm

Or we may use the Oak Harbor Information Skills Rubrics.
http://fno.org/libskill.html

An example follows on the next page.

> **Building Upon Others' Ideas**
> A researcher reads with the intent of extending and augmenting the ideas of others.
>
> 5 - Pushes "found ideas" well beyond their original boundaries
> 3 - Adjusts and elaborates upon "found ideas"
> 1 - Translates and summarizes without adding

3. Consuming Critically

We show our students the pros and cons of using the images and templates available commercially. We show them how much care Madison Avenue may devote to the creation of a single image for an important ad campaign. We engage the students is discovering how a picture is now worth far more than a thousand words. We show them how effective custom images may be worth millions and may cost hundreds of thousands of dollars to produce. We convince them to make their own magic whenever possible.

4. Making Magic

When they need images and ideas to persuade an audience, argue a point, or sell a solution to a problem, students learn they can often produce superior images and better ideas by calling upon their own skills and talents. Rather than turning to the meager collection of workplace images bundled with Word™, they grab a digital camera and schedule visits to the real work place. The clip art would have lacked soul, provided narrow choices, failed to represent their local realities and offered nothing much more than convenience.

Schools should consciously equip students with these skills and talents from the earliest grades. As Peter Minshull demonstrates (see "Beyond Clip Art" at http://fno.org/jun99/draw.html) with a class of Canadian children, with the right support, students can learn to draw images of crabs that are far superior to clip art.

5. Altering Templates

If students use templates, we teach them to modify the templates first, to add personal touches and elements to set their documents apart. Students learn to turn frogs into antelopes.

The danger of relying upon the templates accompanying many software products is a combination of two main problems. On the one hand, the student is relying upon the work of some computer professional who may have absolutely no background in visual design and no talent at all. The templates may be quite mediocre – as is often the reaction to the resume templates bundled with Word™.

The second problem is the surrender to sameness entailed with using templates. Students end up with presentations and documents that are echoes of each other. Applying for a college, they represent themselves as the kid like all the others. Not a powerful sales strategy.

For an extended exploration of how to create persuasive and powerful presentations see the online article, "Scoring Power Points" at http://fno.org/sept00/powerpoints.html

6. Building the New Vertical File

Schools with good librarians are beginning to build online collections of images created by students, either their digital photography or their art work. If students are writing about cats, they may turn to the local file server and select from one thousand images photographed, drawn or painted by their fellow students. If they are writing about steam shovels, they select from 500 online or decide to create their own from scratch.

"They said I had too much soul to model for the clip art office man."

Beware the Wizard

Our ultimate goal is the encouragement of personal magic, powerful and persuasive communication by students who have come to trust their talent to develop original images and ideas.

For an extended exploration of how to create the new vertical file, see the online article at http://fno.org/oct00/vertical.html.

Because the new information landscape is streaming by us at supersonic speeds, we find ourselves working overtime to get our minds around the essential issues, trends, and data of our times. Making meaning is harder than ever before. Quick fixes, wizards, and templates abound as substitutes for deeper understanding, but the ultimate answer to information abundance and degradation is powerful thinking.

Are the foxes lurking and feasting inside the hen house? Must schools face wolves in sheepskin?

There are billions of dollars at stake.

As companies rush forward to help schools network, are school boards, school leaders, and teachers asking enough tough questions about the impact of this commercial wave?

Are schools challenging the value, the neutrality, and the reliability of these new educational partners? Are they sifting through the marketing claims, the hype, and the promises to determine what and who they can trust?

Are principals, teachers, and librarians evaluating the new "digital materials" with the same zeal and care once applied to print materials?

Do schools now question the appropriateness of content saturated or surrounded with advertising as they did when first offered free televisions from Channel One more than a decade back?

Why are so many schools at the youngest levels installing software bundles called "**Office**™?"

Why is there no software program called "**Microsoft School**?"

What do schools sacrifice in the way of objectivity, balance, and value when they allow companies to channel students through educational portals?

What are the pros and cons of running schools with the skills, attitudes, and values of a Firestone, a Microsoft or an Amazon.com?

Billions of Dollars for Connectivity

According to Andrew Trotter, writing in the September 20, 2000 issue of **Education Week**, "Rating the E-rate," the E-rate program has provided 5.1 billion dollars in discounts to support the networking of schools in the United States. Meanwhile, countries such as Singapore, Australia, and Canada have also advanced huge sums.

This rush of computers into classrooms amounts to a flood. Trotter points out that Internet computers are now available in more than a million American classrooms. The pace of change and the torrent of dollars has been remarkable.

Beware the Gray Flannel Trojan Horse

The extent of federal support for such networking is outlined in "E-rate and the Digital Divide: A Preliminary Analysis From the Integrated Studies of Educational Technology," (U.S. Department of Education, September 2000).

Unfortunately, this report illustrates one of the major problems decried throughout this book - the tendency to put cart before horse - funding equipment and infrastructure without adequate corresponding funds for professional and program development.

Most E-Rate Funds Are Used For Internal Connections
The largest share of E-Rate funds (58 percent) has supported the acquisition of equipment and services for internal building connections, while 34 percent is used for telecommunications services, and eight percent is allocated to the cost of Internet access.

"E-rate and the Digital Divide" - Page xi

This surge of hardware and connectivity spending has attracted a legion of salespeople and consultants eager to support school efforts with products, advice, and adult learning programs of various kinds.

Minding One's Own Business

Those who have devoted a lifetime to studying schools and how students learn best should look cautiously at the products and offerings of newcomers and outsiders who may have little or no experience, training, or knowledge of how schools work or children learn.

Unfortunately, many people outside of schools possess little respect for the thinking, the experience, or knowledge of teachers and educators. For decades now, as Larry Cuban (1986) has fully documented, there have been powerful entities outside of schools who have seen new technologies as a way to displace many school practices viewed as ineffective.

Many of the ill-fated reform efforts of the past two decades have originated outside of schools at the insistence of corporate leaders who began offering "help" soon after the release of the 1982 report, "A Nation at Risk." That report sparked a host of proposals to improve schools that often tried to impose business strategies on schools as if they were factories and students were products rolling through a factory. In many cases, these reformers would simply transport greater competition or tougher tests into the educational world as if they could transform schools with a few quick gestures.

Beware the Gray Flannel Trojan Horse

The landscape is littered with failed reform initiatives imposed by state legislatures that have acted without sufficient understanding of how schools might change, often imposing new measures at the behest of corporate thinkers who think they know best.

Dot Compost

When it comes to educational technologies, we are seeing history repeat itself, as legislatures rush to be early and impressive in the networking game, committing huge sums to cable schools and run state networks without heeding the lessons of the past regarding the full cost of implementing such programs.

"Dot Compost" suddenly appeared in the weeks before this book went to press - a term that captures the demise of the fabulous dot.com empires that emerged at the end of the last century but collapsed in this one.

In some states, legislatures have foolishly started networking at the lowest grades where the Internet does the least good and many educators question the value of such technologies.

In other states, nearly all the money has been poured into equipment without supporting professional development. Such actions distort the agenda and may actually slow the pace of improvement.

For several years, state leaders, federal leaders, and major telecommunications and computing companies emphasized connectivity as if an Internet connection in a classroom would automatically work a miracle without addressing all of the other key elements outlined in this book.

Bad Business

In some particularly unfortunate cases, partnerships between state and provincial leaders on the one hand and hardware, software, telecommunications and publishing companies on the other hand direct the design of the learning programs at the very pinnacles of power.

These relationships can promote bad business and worse schooling.

Decisions that shape classroom realities are made far above and far away, then handed down as bundles, packages, contracts, and *faits accomplis*. Many of those involved negotiating these deals have little understanding of schools or children but spout phrases and rhetoric about the knowledge economy or digital generation with the same certainty and arrogance that was typical of dot.com prophets during the end of last century.

How do these packages and deals adversely shape the lives of teachers and students?

In some cases, the leaders contract for professional development with companies that will use an applications training model straight from industry.

The trainers may have never taught children in schools. They teach software. They know **Excel™**. They know **Access™** or **Front Page™**. They use templates and examples from the business world. They know nothing about curriculum . . . less about integration strategies.

They often march through the software skills continuum without customizing the lessons to match the developmental needs or styles of the learners. They know little about adult learning. They know nothing about the value of these software tools within the context of schools.

This is bad business. Worse schooling.

Instead of winning the enthusiastic support of teachers for new technologies and literacy, such partnership may undermine support, provoke cynicism, and slow progress.

Good Schooling?

Sometimes schools will buy rights to educational packages, digital resources and "portals" that may not honor basic educational values. Some violate notions of privacy, decency, and neutrality.

Many software packages are set so that students automatically begin their educational tours through gateways and portals designed by companies to stimulate buying appetites.

Sometimes the portal is more like a gauntlet than a gateway!

As an example of the conflicts of interest implicit in such sites, such advertising and such partnerships, we have one credit card company offering educational materials designed to show young people how to manage their money responsibly!

"Why pay today when you can borrow and delay payment at high interest rates?"

As students cruise through the lists of online resources, the sites often appear within a shell of advertising to match the student inquiry.

This heavy influence of advertising, marketing, and corporate image building stands in stark contrast to educational portals created by librarians such as **KidsClick!**

Beware the Gray Flannel Trojan Horse

http://sunsite.berkeley.edu/KidsClick!/

KidsClick! is a project of the Ramapo Catskill Library System. Unlike most of the commercial portals, there is a clear statement regarding selection policies.

http://www.kidsclick.org/selection.html

An **Education Week Technology Update** on October 20, 1999 listed several companies now offering portals to schools and covered the pros and cons of such sites.

http://www.edweek.org/ew/ewstory.cfm?slug=08tech.h19

The list included INET Library, Inc., Electric SchoolHouse, Inc., FamilyEducation Co., Lycos, Inc., Lightspan Partnership, Inc., Copernicus Interactive, Inc., and ZapMe! Corp.

Some of these ventures promise a great deal but end up disappointing participating schools.

Forbes.Com reported in November of 2000 that "ZapMe Kills Computers In The Classroom." The November 28 article by Betsy Schiffman is available online.

http://biz.yahoo.com/fo/001128/1127zapme.html

Launched in 1996, ZapMe of San Ramon, Calif., wanted to give away free computer equipment and access to U.S. schools. The hitch was that the equipment and access would be supported by banner advertising, a concept frowned upon by educators. Still, ZapMe launched two successful pilot schools in 1998. By the end of the third quarter of 2000, ZapMe had wired 2,300 schools in 45 states, providing approximately 2 million students with Internet access.

Plagued by criticism and disappointing revenues, ZapMe has been forced to take away the "free" part of the program.

The company now has directions at LearningGate.Com explaining how schools may purchase the labs they thought were free. No purchase, no computers!

"Let's keep learning together," the company suggests warmly.

http://www.learningate.com/site/content/lgPromo/default.asp

Some of the commercial sites have a greater focus on shopping than they do on pointing students and educators toward curriculum related materials. While waiting for slow loading educational content pages, banner ads sometimes flash high priority messages grabbing for the attention of the waiting browser.

Beware the Gray Flannel Trojan Horse

Looking for professional development opportunities? One of these portals sends you first to its strategic partners. This is not an "open door policy." More like steerage . . . If you persist and click through several levels, you may find a list of other providers, but the strategic partners remain prominently displayed at the top while all the others are listed farther down the page out of sight with prominent competitors ignored and unmentioned.

Unlike a good library, some of these portal sites unabashedly direct members and visitors to information not because it is the best available but because it is provided by business partners.

Recommendations at some sites are for sale, like shelf space in a grocery store. If you want prominent placement or mention for your product or your information, a company may have to sign a partnership agreement or pay for a high ranking. Payola has become a standard way of doing business in a dot.com world.

Rankings in search engine listings are also for sale at sites like **GoTo** (http://www.goto.com) which has the equivalent of an auction with top ranking for a search such as "educational technology" going to the highest bidder.

What does all this have to do with schools?

The whole notion of "channeling" (steering, directing, leading) runs counter to long-standing traditions of education that argue for independent thought. The minds, preferences, and brand loyalties of young students should not be for sale or for rent by those entrusted with their upbringing.

Stemming the Tide

Even though corporate partnerships are all the rage in some quarters, boards of education and school administrators should remain vigilant and cautious when it comes to marketing intrusions into the learning process.

Most boards have policies prohibiting advertising in schools. This is a good first step, but the incursions have become so subtle and so pervasive for any student browsing the Internet that it is probably impossible to block all advertising unless filters are installed.

The most serious intrusions are those that limit choice and sanction marketing on a large scale. When districts or schools sign agreements with portals or providers that severely restrict access to information and promote brand loyalties as if they were family values, they do their students a great disservice.

"What kind of education did you get?"

Beware the Gray Flannel Trojan Horse

"Windows."
"Mac."
"Ford.
"General Motors."
"General Electric."
"Pepsi."
"Coke."
"Kleenex."
"Amazon."
"Borders."
"Barnes & Noble."
"McDonald's"
"Burger King"

The trends outlined in this chapter are disturbing, Comfortably wrapped in lucrative partnerships of their own, some national organizations that might have been counted on to warn against such "Faustian" deals in the past have sadly "gone over to the other side." They have become cheerleaders and bandwagon proponents rather than protectors of childhood rights and values.

Beware the Shallow Waters!

The Dangers of Ignoring History and the Research on Change in Schools

Even though we have been trying to change schools for a very long time, many of the leaders of the recent drive to network classrooms appear unaware of that history. They show by their actions, their promises, and their strategies that they have little understanding of the failures and mishaps that accompanied many earlier school change efforts.

They appear unaware of educational research that outlines the elements of successful innovations. They seem headed for shallow waters as they emphasize the purchase and installation of equipment while underfunding organizational development and ignoring the lessons of the past.

A History of Virtual Change?

Even though the federal government has funded hundreds of innovations during the past three or more decades, these innovative projects have often proven difficult to replicate, extend, transplant, or prolong.

Virtual change is innovation that fails to take root. We may see much activity and much spinning of wheels, but the spinning of wheels may not take our students very far. The innovation may not translate into a substantial shift in daily classroom practice. Students may not learn more or act more competently.

We must not confuse the presence of "sound and fury" - cables, monitors or Internet "drops" - with real change. We must not assume that dozens of hours on the Internet will enhance student literacy, improve inferential reasoning, or replace older information technologies such as books. We cannot expect that laptops will transform students into better writers simply by virtue of possession. Real change requires much more than the purchase of good equipment.

> "How can it be that so much school reform has taken place over the last century yet schooling appears pretty much the same as it's always been?"
>
> Larry Cuban

Research Example One - Michael Fullan

As perhaps the leading thinker about school change in this decade, Michael Fullan has created a substantial body of writing and research that should guide any school or district asking how to bring new technologies into classrooms successfully.

In **The New Meaning of Educational Change** (1992), Fullan examines the reform efforts of the 1960s, 1970s, and 1980s in order to understand why so many initiatives failed to improve the lives of children and teachers.

Fullan emphasizes the difference between change and progress. Because not all change is for the good, he argues that we should be requiring that the innovation we are considering will actually enhance student performance or well being. In all too many cases, he shows that innovations were chosen for doubtful reasons in the past.

But even good ideas can flounder and innovations founder, according to Fullan, when implementation plans ignore school realities. High on his list of realities would be the factors combining to frustrate or derail most change efforts.

While it is beyond the scope of this chapter to summarize all of Fullan's findings and suggestions, a few examples should suffice to whet project leaders' appetites for a thorough reading of his work.

Beware the Shallow Waters

1) Fullan: *The daily press (the need to take care of moment to moment classroom pressures) is a mammoth obstacle to be overcome if an innovation is ever going to take root.*

> Teachers are often constrained from thinking about new ways of organizing learning in their classrooms by the need to handle day to day issues, surprises, crises, and challenges.
>
> (Fullan's summary of research by
> both Huberman and Crandall, pp. 33-34).

Wherever schools are networking or launching major reform efforts such as standards-based curriculum drives, teachers lament that there is never enough time, yet planners often ignore the entire issue of the daily press as if good teachers will simply shrug it off.

So what? Buying lots of equipment without addressing the daily press is a dangerous strategy. Making robust use of networked computers requires many demanding changes from teachers that they are unlikely to welcome or embrace unless the district has provided some relief from the daily press.

2) Fullan: *Those who ignore the social and cultural realities of schools while launching and implementing projects are not likely to make much progress.*

Fullan emphasizes the need for addressing the subjective meaning of change (how it feels to participants) as well as the objective meaning of change (the key elements that may contribute to what Fullan terms "a change in practice.")

So what? Many schools have spent their entire technology budget on hardware and infrastructure. The most successful implementations will devote major funding to professional development designed to help staff modify their teaching strategies, learning strategies and belief systems.

3) Fullan: *Some designs and strategies have worked for change much more effectively than others and we now possess the basis for wise choices.*

From the history of school change efforts, Fullan extracts powerful lessons and design principles that should inform the planning of those who would network schools. In succeeding chapters, he lays out four simplified stages for the change process.

So what? Every district technology plan should explicitly address the change process in a balanced manner and lay out an approach that is solidly anchored in what we know about effective strategies.

4) Fullan: *Planning must be incredibly flexible and responsive to the actual experience, changing along with discoveries and surprises (of which there will be many).*

> "Many proposals for change strike them (teachers) as frivolous - they do not address issues, psychic rewards, time scheduling, student disruption, interpersonal support and so forth"

In his Chapter Six, Fullan shows that many school reform efforts fail because the participants lack an understanding of change. He offers ten assumptions about change that should be well understood by participants and leaders alike.

So what? The most impressive returns on hardware investments will be won by those districts that define the venture as a change in the school's culture for learning rather than the mere equipping of class-rooms with computers.

Unfortunately, few district technology plans look beyond hard-ware and physical resources in a manner consistent with Fullan's advice.

Research Example Two - Larry Cuban

Larry Cuban, currently a professor of education at Stanford, has provided important insight into school change by describing the often disappointing history of various attempts to bring new technologies into schools.

In his 1986 study, Cuban outlined the experience of schools with each succeeding wave of "miracle workers" - radio, film, television, computers - and provided hypotheses for why these tools failed to penetrate or transform classrooms to any great extent.

Beware the Shallow Waters

More recently, Cuban has been a steady voice challenging the least tenable assumptions of technologists and the exaggerated marketing claims of vendors. In an excellent 1998 article available online, Cuban teams with Kirkpatrick to summarize and characterize the findings of research on the effectiveness of new technologies.

The authors report that some evidence of (mild) benefits from computer assisted instruction (CAI and CMI) emerged from meta studies but indicate that there were few convincing, well designed studies of "computer enhanced instruction" (CEI) - an approach requiring substantial teacher skill.

Research Example Three - Ellen Mandinach

One of the best documented efforts to explore the potential of new technologies to make change is the **Systems Thinking and Curriculum Innovation Network Project** (STACIN) developed by Ellen Mandinach and her team at ETS, a project that tracked the use of a software program called STELLA™, a simulation-modeling package. The project extended for more than six years with six high schools and two middle schools.

Beware the Shallow Waters

Despite careful planning, a well designed training program, and a very thoughtful implementation strategy, the researchers candidly reported that the introduction of systems thinking with STACIN took a long time, required considerable patience, and worked best with teachers who were willing to tolerate a high degree of student control and surprise.

In a paper presented at AERA in 1992, "The Impact of Technological Innovation on Teaching and Learning Activities," Mandinach reports that movement in stage from survival, to mastery, and then to impact (which means substantial infusion into the classroom activities) is much harder for some types of teachers than others.

Regrettably, the STACIN experience bolsters Cuban's pessimistic forecast for the chances of a fundamental shift in the use of technologies within schools.

So what? We are left with a real quandary . . . If we determine that this generation of students needs to be educated by "a guide on the side," not "a sage on the stage," what do we do with all the sages who refuse to be guides?

We have excellent models at hand from researchers like Mandinach to guide willing teachers comfortably from one stage to another if they are willing, but we have not confronted the challenge of those who will not spare any change. Can we convert sages into guides? Have we created professional development models that will make this transition likely? For an online article about reaching such teachers, go to http://fno.org/sum99/reluctant.html.

Research Example Four - Steven Hodas

In his 1993 essay and review of the literature, "Technology Refusal and the Organizational Culture of Schools," Steven Hodas suggests that the purposes of many technologies run counter to the true or embedded purposes of schools, that they are rejected not so much because of flawed implementation plans as because these technologies seem alien to many of the teachers and administrators.

http://olam.ed.asu.edu/epaa/v1n10.html

This paper proposes that technology is never neutral: that its values and practices must always either support or subvert those of the organization into which it is placed; and that the failures of technology to alter the look-and-feel of schools more generally result from a mismatch between the values of school organization and those embedded within the contested technology.

Hodas points out that schools are themselves a "technology" for the delivery of learning and can rapidly organize to resist pressures for new technologies, especially if the workers within the schools cannot recognize value behind the new offerings.

So what? Technology planners must not fall into the trap of thinking that classroom practice will change simply because we have changed the equipment in the room. If a majority of teachers in a school are intent upon covering curriculum content to score well on new state standards and tests, networked information technologies may be greeted with refusal and resistance rather than enthusiasm and adoption.

Research Example Five - Henry Becker

Henry J. Becker and his team have been surveying teachers across the United States to find out how they report their use of the Internet and other technology learning experiences.

Becker's studies have found that uses of the Internet and new technologies vary dramatically according to a teacher's philosophy and practice. Based on surveys of teachers across the nation, Becker contrasts the reported attitudes and practices of "traditional" teachers with others he calls "constructivist" teachers. (1999)

Teachers who believe strongly that good teaching involves facilitating independent student work rather than emphasizing direct instruction and skills practice, and who put those beliefs into practice, along with an emphasis on complex thinking, were much more likely to have their students use the Internet than were those who put relatively limited value on such approaches to teaching.

In addition, these teachers, whom he labels "constructivist," were twice as likely to believe the Internet in the classroom to be essential to their teaching as those who were least constructivist. Similarly, for teacher Internet use, the most constructivist teachers (19% of all teachers) were two-and-one-half times as likely as the most traditional teachers (the 22% closest to the "traditional" end of the scale) to use the Internet for their own professional use.

So what? These are troubling findings given the current popularity of distributing computers evenly across classrooms in twos, threes and fours. Even though we have evidence that teacher commitment to use varies dramatically across teacher types, planners seem to be ignoring the evidence, hoping, perhaps, that the presence of computers will change their minds. While Becker is curious to determine if such transformations will occur, he reports no conclusive evidence of such changes.

67

Beware the Shallow Waters

Given the preference of most teachers in Becker's survey for "traditional" teaching strategies and their expressed concerns about state testing pressures, his report should raise eyebrows if it could just gain more widespread attention.

Most teachers (64%) report themselves to be more comfortable teaching in a traditional style than a constructivist one (28%), and more believe that even students prefer that type of instruction (53% to 37%) even though they believe that constructivist teaching is better for students in helping them gain useful skills.

We must not underestimate the difficulty of moving toward constructivist classrooms, as an excellent article by Mark Windschitl in the June, 1999 issue of **Phi Delta Kappan** explains:

> Constructivism is premised on the belief that learners actively create, interpret, and reorganize knowledge in individual ways.
> . . . students should participate in experiences that accommodate these ways of learning.
> . . . before teachers and administrators adopt such practices, they should understand that constructivism cannot make its appearance in the classroom as a set of isolated instructional methods grafted on otherwise traditional teaching techniques.
>
> page 752

The journey from traditional to student centered teaching is one that is rarely addressed by technology advocates and even more rarely funded, but new approaches to professional development offer hope.

"It can't be done."

Amy looked at the phone in her hand and wished she had the network supervisor - Sam Peters - in the same room with her.

"What do you mean, it can't be done?" she pressed.

"Trust me," he answered back. "Do you have any idea how long our job list has grown since September 1? These teachers come back from summer vacation and all kinds of problems develop."

As librarian of a large high school in the Midwest, Amy was eager to expand the number of information products available to her students to support their curriculum inquiries. She had devoted summer weeks with teachers identifying information resources to purchase that would help the school to address the state curriculum standards and tests.

Now she was being blocked by the one person she needed the most. She had ordered subscriptions and paid for site licenses. Now she needed the products installed on one of the high school's three file servers. She also needed the software clients for each product installed on each of the 375 desktops in her school.

"No way I could get to that before next year," Sam continued, evidently interpreting her silence as disbelief. "We have so much compliance work to finish to keep the state off our backs, and the Business Office is really nervous about the integrity of payroll and student records."

Amy had heard most of these complaints before, just about any time she asked for anything out of the ordinary. And she knew that Sam was cruelly understaffed . . . that the district had only two "technicians" to support more than 2000 desktops. So she decided to offer help.

"How about we do it ourselves, then?" she volunteered. "I know that Peter Freedman, Joyce Chung, and I could do the fileserver installations, and we could also create a team of volunteers to reach out and touch all the desktops."

There was a long silence at Sam's end of the phone . . . and then a sigh. "I can't have you doing that, Amy. You know I have a policy forbidding any installations by folks outside my department. It just messes things up and creates havoc."

Network Starvation Defined

While the names have been changed, the above tale is true - a story that probably repeats itself in dozens of districts daily across the land. It is a story recurring frequently in other countries such as New Zealand, Australia, Canada, and Sweden. When I share it with audiences, I am amazed by the large percentage of heads nodding in recognition.

The story is an example of **Network Starvation** - the dramatic failure to provide enough technical staff to support the ongoing use and development of an educational network. It is a serious problem undercutting the success of networks in thousands of districts, but one that goes virtually unnoticed and unmentioned in the press and scholarly work. This understaffing is one of the main reasons we are seeing disappointing reports regarding teachers' use of networks.

The failure to hire adequate technical staff has the effect of limiting the reliability and the curriculum value of networks. It also restricts the level of services provided and functions made available to both staff and students.

Indicators of Network Starvation

How can you tell if your school and your network are suffering from Network Starvation? Check off whether many of the following indicators are typical of your situation.

Yes or No Indicators of Network Starvation

- Technicians are responsible for 500+ computers each.
- There are no networked information products available on desktops (such as periodicals or encyclopedias).

- Educational staff is not provided storage space on the network.
- Students are not allowed storage space on the network.
- Service problems take weeks before they are fixed.
- Educational staff is not allowed to design storage areas or menus on the network.
- Students are not allowed to have e-mail accounts on the network.
- No one is allowed to install any program except the network staff.
- Most fileserver management, including Web pages and Web serving, is handled centrally by network staff without teachers or librarians being allowed direct access.
- When educational staff members request augmented services, they often hear "It cannot be done."
- The network freezes up and stops working at least once each day.
- After new versions of software programs arrive in the district, it takes 4-6 months before they appear on desktops.

Diminished Reliability

As we seek to broaden the percentage of teachers who employ new technologies to support classroom learning on a daily or weekly basis, network reliability is a critically important issue. While early adopters may have a high tolerance for surprise and disappointment, late adopting, skeptical teachers have almost no tolerance for unreliable networks and may use breakdowns as a rationale for holding back. Wanting to feel prepared and highly effective, and being mindful of enormous pressures to meet curriculum standards, they are (rightly) reluctant to mess around with something that is "hit or miss."

Failure to staff at a full level (one technician for 250-500 desktops) puts a network at risk and contributes to instability. Small problems grow into large ones. Crisis management becomes the main way of operating. The thinly stretched team of technicians goes from fire to fire and crisis to crisis often relying on "work arounds" and Band-Aids rather than long term, sound solutions.

Failure to staff adequately undermines the value of the huge investment made in computers and networking.

Network Starvation

Diminished Curriculum Value

A network is only half of a product. It is a bit like plumbing. Unless something flows through the network that relates to the curriculum and is organized in ways that will appeal to a broad cross section of teachers, the network will seem irrelevant and frivolous to serious teachers who are quick to criticize the "free" Internet for its lack of reliability, organization, and content.

Those districts who offer nothing on the desktop other than software and the Internet will face serious skepticism on the part of teachers. Too few district decision-makers understand how much technical staff is required to "develop" a network. They tend to think primarily of installation. They do not realize that installation is only the first quarter of the ball game.

After installation we should enjoy an information feast.

Diminished Services and Functions

We invest in networks so that students may communicate globally and conduct research with a rich assortment of electronic information resources, but in all too many districts, the failure to hire enough technicians blocks many student and staff uses. It is a bit like buying a Rolls Royce but holding back the money for a set of tires. It may look pretty sitting up on blocks in front of the house, but you should not expect to travel far.

Districts that fail to staff appropriately are buying a limo without gas for the tank, tires for the road, or oil for the transmission. They find themselves without storage for students or staff, without student e-mail accounts, without rich information resources, and without much hands-on development by educators. Understaffed technical departments are prone to emphasize control and restriction as a survival tactic.

The Competition is Fierce

Even if schools wanted to hire many more technicians, they are in short supply. The business world, while acknowledging the need for much more generous staffing levels (1 technician for every 100 computers), is having a very hard time finding them. The January 1, 1998 Issue of **CIO Magazine** outlines the "staffing crisis" in some detail in "Desperate Times, Creative Measures." http://www.cio.com/archive/

Network Starvation

010198_over_content.html

These businesses are often able to offer much more attractive packages than school districts so that skilled technicians are hard to find and unlikely to stay in underpaying school districts long.

It turns out that setting appropriate staffing levels is only the first step in a very difficult process. Finding and holding onto skilled technicians is hard for any employer.

Helpful Resources

One of the most thorough studies outlining district staffing needs is an Arizona Technology in Education Alliance white paper, "Staffing for Technology Support" at

http://www.aztea.org/resources/whitepaper/staffing.htm.

This 1997 white paper by Hank Stabler of the Peoria School District in Glendale, Arizona provides a formula to help calculate the number of F.T.E.s required. For example . . .

1000 workstations, 2,000 users, 30 clusters (e.g. school offices), 25 applications supported, 3 operating systems (OS400, Windows 95 and Mac), and licenses required for 25 different software packages. The staffing would be determined as follows.

$$HR = 1000/500 + 2000/1000 + 30/15 + 25/50 + 25/25 + 3/1$$
$$HR = 2 + 2 + 2 + .5 + 1 + 3 \text{ (for a total of 10.5 FTE)}$$

The formula is based on Arfman, J. and Roden, P. (1992). "Project Athena: Supporting Distributed Computing at MIT." IBM System Journal, v. 31, n. 3, pp. 550-563.

The Network Manifesto

Who controls the network resources and design process in your school district and school? Is it a balanced team with representation from teachers, librarians, school administrators and IT folks? Or is control and management tilted to one extreme or another?

Do the educators have so much influence and hands-on control that the integrity and the performance of the network is threatened?

Or conversely, do the network and IT folks have so much influence and hands-on control that the curriculum value of the network is throttled?

Take the quiz on the next page to see if your network has a strong educational focus.

Network Starvation

Rate your situation from 0 stars to 4 stars on each of the beliefs below.

0 stars No evidence of this belief in practice at all.
1 star   Some promising statements but mostly lip service.
2 stars Occasional evidence that the belief is practiced.
3 stars Frequent signs that the belief is practiced.
4 stars The belief is fully operationalized and practiced
with consistency and vigor.

The Network Manifesto:
Beliefs to Create Vibrant Networks
Serving Literacy and Learning

Rating

____ 1) **Information Richness** - Networks support learning most powerfully when they provide rich information matched to the district and state curriculum standards.

____ 2) **Developmental Match** - Networks support learning most fully when they offer rich information suited to the developmental needs of students.

____ 3) **User Friendliness** - Networks support learning most effectively when they are designed with menus and user interfaces that are appropriate for the age and the learning styles of students using them.

____ 4) **Focus on Learning** - Those with classroom experience and training in information science and learning theories (teachers and librarians) should have a determining voice in the design of the school and district information systems.

____ 5) **Educator Management** - One or two responsible, designated educational staff members at each school should be granted hands-on access to the file server(s) in each building to make sure there are robust public resources and directories offered to all students in the building.

____ 6) **Educator Preparation** - The district should provide substantial training to teachers and librarians within each building to perform basic network management, design, and development tasks.

Network Starvation

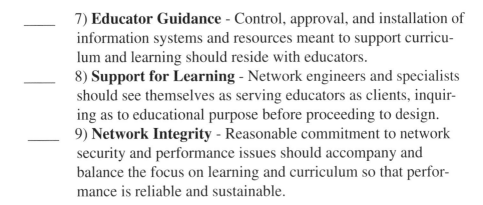

_____ 7) **Educator Guidance** - Control, approval, and installation of information systems and resources meant to support curriculum and learning should reside with educators.

_____ 8) **Support for Learning** - Network engineers and specialists should see themselves as serving educators as clients, inquiring as to educational purpose before proceeding to design.

_____ 9) **Network Integrity** - Reasonable commitment to network security and performance issues should accompany and balance the focus on learning and curriculum so that performance is reliable and sustainable.

"I've pulled the plug," Juanita announced.

Juanita is an early adopter. Way back in the early 1980s, she grasped the potential of personal computers and did everything possible to blend their use into her classroom.

She began with Basic, teaching her students simple programming. Then she tried **Logo™** and **Lego Logo™** as computers became more user friendly, and she managed to beg borrow and steal a half dozen PCs for her classroom.

Juanita was a pioneer with word processing in the mid-eighties as she showed her students how to compose their compositions from start to finish on the computer. By the end of that decade, she had bought her first classroom modem, moved to the high school, and experimented with electronic mail and online research.

By the time the Internet caught on as a mass phenomenon in the mid nineties, Juanita and her students were already veterans. They had been surfing the Net long before Netscape and AOL became household terms and high flying Internet stocks.

Juanita was a pioneer, an enthusiast, an experimenter, and a cheerleader for new technologies in schools. As each new wave of software and equipment arrived with golden promises of school reform and transformation, Juanita was quick to learn, to adapt, to integrate, and to embrace the new tools.

Until recently . . .

"I just stopped in my tracks one day," she explains to her long term teaching buddy, Frank. "I pulled out the plug. I turned off the machines."

Because Frank has marveled at Juanita's technology heroics for more than two decades, he shakes his head skeptically.

"You?"

Juanita is determined to explain. "It's nothing permanent," she says. "I just decided it was time to stop and take stock, to ask what matters. Time to shed, prune, and discard. Time to put my program on track. I just started to wonder how all this connectivity was actually contributing to my students' understanding of Shakespeare, Thoreau, and their own poetry."

The Unplugged Classroom

"You know how artists suddenly issued unplugged performances? That's what I'm doing. I'm pulling the plug. Going acoustic. Just for a week or two."

The Growth of Skepticism

Even as many schools are struggling to enlist late adopting, reluctant teachers who report insufficient training and little inclination to make use of networked technologies, they may also note a growth of healthy skepticism on the part of early adopters like Juanita who were quick to try out new technologies in the past.

Once the equipment is installed and the network connects students and teachers to the rest of the world, well meaning, conscientious teachers may rightfully ask tough questions like these:

1) Will a network improve the power of my students' writing?
2) Will a network deepen my students' understanding of the key concepts mandated by the curriculum I must cover?
3) Will these new tools increase my students' ability to read, write and reason?
4) If I allow students to spend hundreds of hours on this network, what do I remove from my program? How do I make time?
5) Which activities have been proven most effective?
6) What are the biggest obstacles I must overcome to make these tools work effectively. Which strategies will succeed?
7) When is a PowerPoint presentation worth doing?
8) Will the network help me meet the curriculum standards?
9) Why won't they let students have e-mail or storage on the network?
10) How do I manage with just two or three computers in my classroom?

These questions should precede the installation of a network throughout a school, but they are rarely addressed or publicly honored in the present climate either before or after installation. Unfortunately, such questions may be greeted and then dismissed as heresy by those who have rushed forward to run cables to classrooms with little thought of student learning.

The Unplugged Classroom

The Primacy of Program Development

Previous chapters have clarified the dangers of underfunding the professional development required to prepare teachers for meaningful use of networks.

Unfortunately, professional development without program development is a bit like learning to play the violin without sheet music.

Acquiring technique may lead to some use, but technique without clarity of educational purpose and philosophy may lead to bad practice and silly uses as described in Jane Healy's book, **Failure to Connect** (1999).

At a recent national conference I watched several teachers proudly stand up to display PowerPoint presentations created by their students.

"This report was really long," commented one teacher (as if length were a good thing), apologizing for cutting it back to a few sample slides.

"And I must apologize for messing up the animation. He had the animal moving across the screen just wonderfully, but I messed it up."

I watched members of the audience drift away as superficial, glitzy work was held up as an example of digital progress. There was plenty of flash, plenty of razzle-dazzle, but little evidence of careful thought and deep content. It was an old fashioned encyclopedia report slimmed down and dressed up with lots of clip art and special effects. Transitions, sound effects, and extreme fonts were used whenever possible.

By introducing lots of notebook computers, these teachers and these schools had managed to integrate new technologies into the daily life of students, but to what good purpose? It was hard to see value.

Powerpointing can be pointless if schools fail to emphasize the essential elements of deep research on essential questions, if they do not show students the traits of effective communication, and if they do not focus on value added.

The Primacy of Effective Teaching

For the past two decades, most schools put their energy into training teachers to use software.

They should have devoted far more time to strategic issues - those central to good teaching and effective learning with such tools.

We fell into the trap of thinking the software and the tools would make better readers, writers, thinkers, and communicators without adding the yeast of good teaching to the technology loaf. We ended up with flat bread.

We have growing evidence from Hank Becker (1999) and **Education Week** (Trotter, 1999) that little use may occur unless teachers introduce new technologies with scaffolding (structure) and support to bring about intelligent and thoughtful use.

From the very start, scaffolded lessons provide examples of quality work done by others. Right from the beginning, students are shown rubrics and standards that define excellence.

In traditional school research, students were often kept in the dark until the product was completed.

Without clearly stated criteria, it was difficult to know what constituted quality work. Is it a matter of length? the number of sources cited? Does originality count? Does the logic and coherence of the argument matter? What constitutes adequate evidence?

There are at least a dozen issues, all of which deserve attention and elaboration. As an example, consider the online rubrics for successful multimedia reports available at

http://www2.ncsu.edu/ncsu/cep/midlink/rub.multi.htm

One example follows:

Rubric for Originality & Inventiveness

1 The work is a meager collection or rehash of other people's ideas, products, images and inventions. There is no evidence of new thought.

2 The work is an extensive collection and rehash of other people's ideas, products, images and inventions. There is no evidence of new thought or inventiveness.

3 The product shows evidence of originality and inventiveness. While based on an extensive collection of other people's ideas, products, images and inventions, the work extends beyond that collection to offer new insights.

4 The product shows impressive evidence of originality and inventiveness. The majority of the content is fresh, original and inventive.

The Unplugged Classroom

Beyond Skepticism to Value

Unless schools emphasize all three key elements - 1) program development, 2) professional development and 3) effective teaching - with new technologies, they run the risk of fostering the skepticism of early adopters as well as late adopters.

The technology binge proceeded far too long with inadequate attention to what we know about learning and teaching. Smart schools will slow down the wiring and buying process in order to place greater priority on the invention of effective classroom lessons designed to address state standards and improve student performance.

It is arguably more effective to buy fewer computers and then move them around strategically in order to concentrate on value.

There is little profit for schools in rushing out to buy computers for every classroom. The mere act of purchase and installation does not transform classroom practice by itself. We must put our program horses before our technology carts, stressing information literacy.

Chapter 11 - What's the Story Here?

Our stories can help shape who we are and where we are going. But in all too many cases, there is no shared, intended story to inspire a school to make good use of new technologies. In many cases, stories are more like rumors than effective elements in a planned change initiative.

> **School Story One**
>
> This school takes children far. We're like a family here. We expect every child to learn and grow - to reach out for some kind of personal truth and some kind of personal victory.
>
> We don't care whether they are doctors' kids or homeless. They are all God's children . . . gifted, talented, and remarkable in some way.
>
> It is our job to help each one bloom and flourish, to walk through life with head held high. We're fond of sandboxes and play. Sometimes we use pails and shovels. Sometimes we visit other countries with e-mail.

Story creating and telling should be a basic tool of any group trying to build good new futures. Some call this activity scenario building. Others call it myth building. Still others call it visioning.

But there is some danger that story creating and telling might wander too far from its agrarian roots and take on a gray flannel aspect that might steer the story into quicksand.

The best stories are rooted in soulful human realities, the soil and the loam of dreams. They are personal, compelling, and quite concrete in their details and examples. Good stories can make you smell, touch, and taste what is about to happen.

What's the Story Here?

Traits of Effective Stories

The story tells

- Who we are.
- What we care about.
- Where we are going.
- Why we are going there.
- How we are going.
- What choices are available.
- What we will do if trouble strikes.
- How we will learn as we go.
- How we will keep open minded.
- How we will know we have arrived.
- How we will celebrate.

The Emperor's New Clothes serves as a warning of story telling gone awry. Threadbare realities and naked truths abound.

"Story" and associated words such as "legend" and "myth," have an assortment of traditional and modern meanings that can almost contradict each other at times.

In general, the traditional meanings of these words tend to be more pure and innocent than the modern meanings. The comments below attempt to draw attention to these differences. In these days of spin, the natural tendency of story tellers to enhance or exaggerate has risen to new levels of distortion and misinformation.

Important Definitions

Story

In its pure, traditional meaning, a story is a rather factual account of something that happened. But even from the earliest of times, story tellers have seen the audience impact of exaggeration and dramatization, so the original events may take on extra shine in the words of the story teller.

Then there are stories and plays that are fiction from the beginning, accounts that are make-believe, like **Hamlet** or **Macbeth** or **Jack and the Beanstalk**.

Given the potential of stories to sway the hearts and minds of listeners, they have always held promise for those who would like to control and influence others, so they have been favorite tools of propagandists, demagogues, and marketing gurus. They have used stories to generate spin and stir up the emotions of whatever group is worth inspiring (today, tomorrow, or next week.)

At its worst, the word "story" has come to mean "lie."

"He made up a story to cover his tracks."

"Likely story!"

We have even seen a shift in the meaning of a "news story" as facts have become an increasingly less important aspect of reporting while entertainment and tabloid values have shifted coverage and ethics both.

Legend

Legends were somewhat fanciful stories meant to help explain the past or to transmit important beliefs. They were usually thought to be partially historical, as in the legend of the Trojan Horse or the Arthurian legend of the Holy Grail.

During modern times, legends have descended into a different type of use, as the cult of celebrities raises baseball players and actors and corporate leaders into legendary status.

"She was a legend in her own time."

The **Original Roget's Thesaurus of English Words** associates "legend" with an interesting list of other words, each of which has proven useful to those who wish to influence the thinking and actions of others:

metaphor: fable, legend, parable, teaching

Myth

In the beginning, myths were stories that helped to explain the beginning of the earth and the meaning of life, among other things. They usually involved a cast of characters ranging from major gods and goddesses down through ranks of lesser deities to mere humans and monsters of various kinds, starting with heroes like Hercules and monsters like Scylla and Charybdis.

Myths could transmit the most important values of the culture and help to define what it meant to be heroic. In some cases they helped to explain the inexplicable.

The poets were not alone in sanctioning myths, for long before the poets, the states and the lawmakers had sanctioned them as a useful expedient . . . They needed to control the people by superstitious fears, and these cannot be aroused without myths and marvels.

Strabo

What's the Story Here?

But myths have taken on new meanings in contemporary times, moving as with stories into more questionable terrain, as myths frequently refer to false versions of reality or the twisted beliefs of some ideology.

> The enemy of the truth is very often not the lie - deliberate, contrived, and dishonest - but the myth - persistent, persuasive and unrealistic.
> John F. Kennedy

In some cases, myths become part of a marketing strategy. Eager to sell laptop computers to schools, for example, many companies paint rosy pictures of the mostly unsubstantiated benefits of buying notebook computers for every student.

It is not the purchase of the machine that works wonders so much as the wondrous activities launched by teachers when they have been supported in learning how to launch best practices.

Those who trumpet the miracles of the machine subtly undermine the case for spending money on good teaching. Myths retain the power to do good and to inspire good works when they are tied to authentic possibilities, when they "ring true." But myths become blather when they herald a new age of wonders and marvels that are supposed to accompany the purchase of various products.

> Time spent on the Net is not passive time, it's active time. It's reading time. It's investigation time. It's skill development and problem-solving time. It's time analyzing, evaluating. It's composing your thoughts time. It's writing time.
> Don Tapscott
> **Growing Up Digital**

To claim that wired schools automatically improve the learning of students is one of the great modern myths. Wiring and equipping are an insufficient recipe for success. Without a well funded, substantial, and strategic commitment to ongoing professional development and technical support, schools are likely to end up with the screensaver's disease, not a surge in student performance.

"Preparing Teachers For the Digital Age," by Andrew Trotter writing for **Technology Counts '99**, a report issued each year until 2000 by **Education Week**, comments as follows:

And a new Education Week survey has found that the typical teacher still mostly dabbles in digital content, using it as an optional ingredient to the meat and potatoes of instruction.

Almost two-thirds of teachers say they rely on software or Web sites for instruction "to a minimal extent" or "not at all.

School Story Two

We have the latest equipment, the fastest network, and every technological advantage imaginable. Every student has a notebook computer, a Web page, and an electronic portfolio.

We prepare them for a digital future by making school into something like a digital stadium.

We expect them to do digital high jumps, broad jumps, and sprints. We present them with a digital decathlon that will challenge the best of them.

Net generation? You betcha! There is no risk here of a digital divide. Our students are fully accomplished digerati even before reaching high school. They know their way around the digital landscape and will graduate with digital capital as well as intellectual capital. Students leave here with the digital equivalent of stock options.

Sometimes the real story is embedded as subtext - lines of truth running like footnotes under the official version.

Planning for robust, integrated use of new technologies in regular classrooms is distinct from planning their installation. Plugging in, it turns out, is much easier than playing!

Much network planning for schools ignores the most important (human) aspects and fails to address either the learning or the program issues that should precede the introduction of hardware and cables.

Sometimes the real story circulates in the staff rooms or out at the front of the school where parents and teachers swap stories.

Healthy planning for change starts with a clear focus on purpose and then proceeds to identify the key elements and steps required to bring about meaningful adaptation of daily practice.

What's the Story Here?

School Story Three

This is about keeping up with the school district next door. They networked before we did, so now we race to do it bigger and better.

The superintendent is off presenting at some national technology conference announcing all kinds of amazing achievements - students learning anywhere and anytime.

When you walk down the hallways, there's lots of equipment, but not much is being used.

School looks like it did last year . . . and the year before that.

Did they invest in professional development? Hire lots of technicians to support the network? Spend money on electronic subscriptions?

Not likely. We were playing catch up. The main thing was being networked. Fast!

The creation of shared stories can be an especially powerful way to provide a clear focus on purpose.

Oftentimes, shared stories emerge from extended dialogue and group exploration over time. The dialogue may focus on particular metaphors that invite repeated visits and consideration.

School Story Four

The West Linn-Wilsonville School District in Oregon provides a vivid example of this planning process and story creating, as the school community first agreed upon major belief statements - bold stroke values - that should guide the thinking of all making plans for the future learning of students in the district.

By clarifying their aspirations, the contributing stake-holders and the School Directors were setting in motion a steering mechanism that would help groups attend to essential matters.

Several years after the adoption of these belief statements, a committee met over many months to plan program changes to match the renovation of one of the district's two high schools.

A metaphor (like porch sitting) may help to translate complexities and abstractions into much more compelling images that are more likely to inspire commitment, engagement, and belief.

In this district, porch sitting became an effective way to focus attention on the methods that people use to think (collectively) about the most challenging questions of life.

"Porches" and "porch sitting" became central metaphors for the new building and the kinds of thinking and learning the district hopes to inspire.

Pondering takes time and fares poorly at hyperspeeds.

Creating Good Stories on Purpose

Good stories should not happen entirely by accident, although some serendipity is often welcome and desirable.

The purpose of this chapter was to heighten awareness of how good stories might prove powerful tools for planning and steering.

Each school and each district may create stories that help the educational communities join together in purposeful, rich partnerships to promote learning, growth, and exploration.

Chapter 12 - How Teachers Learn Technology Best

Note: This chapter is an updated synthesis since the book with this same title was published in 1999.

When it comes to teachers learning and valuing the effective use of new technologies, some schools are discovering that the kinds of training programs offered in the past may not represent the most generative method of reaching a full range of teachers and their students. As mentioned earlier, the key term is "generative" - meaning that behaviors and daily practice will be changed for the better as a consequence of the professional development experience.

Fortunately, some schools are now identifying approaches more likely to encourage teachers to employ these technologies on a frequent and sustained basis to enhance student learning.

Lead districts are finding that adult learning, curriculum development projects and informal support structures are proving powerful in promoting recurrent use aimed at deep curriculum integration.

After two decades of providing software classes to teachers, we need to explore different approaches – those honoring key principles of adult learning while placing both curriculum and literacy ahead of software and technology.

As will be explained later, adult learning strategies are fundamentally different from training strategies and usually more promising because they are tailored to the learning styles, preferences and needs of teachers in ways more likely to win their commitment than the approach more typical of training models.

As noted throughout this book, in some places, eager planners have "put the cart before the horse" - emphasizing the purchase and installation of equipment without providing sufficient funding for the staff learning required to win a reasonable return on the huge investments being made.

We have evidence from Market Data Retrieval (MDR) (1999) that the majority of American teachers enjoy fewer than five hours of technology related professional development annually, and most of that seems to be training.

This challenge is about using new tools to help students master the key concepts and skills embedded in the science, social studies, art, and other curriculum standards. It is not so much about powerpointing, spreadsheeting or word processing. The focus should be on teaching and learning strategies that make a difference in daily practice – on activities translating into stronger student performance. As a result of these practices and the use of these new tools, students should be able to . . .

- Read, reason and write more powerfully.
- Communicate productively with members of a global community.
- Conduct thoughtful research into the important questions, choices and issues of their times.
- Make sense of a confusing world and a swelling tide of information.
- Perform well on the new, more demanding state tests requiring inferential reasoning.

This chapter outlines how teachers learn technology best and how districts may promote such learning to avoid "the screensavers disease" - the failure to use new technologies frequently and meaningfully.

Defining the Challenges

While it is tempting to make frequent usage of technology the goal of professional development, schools should focus efforts on promoting usage that is curriculum rich and likely to make a discernible difference in student achievement.

There is some risk that new technologies may unintentionally lead to slick student performances that are both glib and thin.

When networks enter schools, they often bring with them a flood of information that is shaped, in part, by pop culture and some of the tabloid values typical of some modern media. At its worst, information from the Internet can be either disneyfied or distorted.

Without a focus on sound educational principles, learning with these new technologies can induce a kind of cut-and-paste thinking that might actually undermine the ability of students to think.

It makes sense to start with curriculum and student learning as the clear purpose for the network. Schools create standards-based activities that employ whatever technologies make sense . . . books, e-mail, Web sites, whatever. Learning is the goal. Technologies are mere delivery systems.

The true challenge of professional development is to inspire and prepare classroom teachers to launch these curriculum rich activities with the tools that make sense.

Evidence of Shortfalls

The evidence mounts that few American teachers feel adequately prepared for the challenge of using new technologies in any fashion, not to mention the challenge of using technologies to support curriculum rich, standards-based lessons.

MDR reported in 1999 that about 60% of a national survey of teachers claimed five hours or less of training annually, and yet this chapter argues that training is not the right approach to inspire teachers to make meaningful use of networks. We see too little time devoted in the wrong way to the wrong goal. We need more time and resources applied in the right way to the right tasks.

Hank Becker's research shows that the preferred teaching strategies and styles of teachers usually determine or shape their patterns of technology usage. Those he calls "traditional" teachers are far less apt to allow students to use new technologies than "constructivist" teachers even when they have five or more networked computers in their classrooms.

Becker's research points to the need to do much more than teach technology skills to teachers. We must also convince them of the value of engaging students in problem-based or project-based learning with these new tools. One hundred additional hours of learning computer software is not likely to transform traditional teachers into constructivist teachers.

The transformation of teaching styles, preferences, and behaviors requires persuasion, learning by experience, and the provision of highly personalized learning journeys.

How Teachers Learn

Weakness of Past Efforts and the Training Model

Schools have relied too long on training models and have put too much emphasis on the learning of software. The training model usually involves a march through a series of skill lessons with little adjustment made for learning styles, developmental stages or personal preferences. Because the skills are often learned out of context, they seem remote from classroom practice and leave many teachers wondering about their utility and worth.

What makes this training model even worse in some cases is the use of generic examples for practice that widen the gap even further for the teacher who is asking "How can I use this tool to teach fifth grade social studies?"

Generic examples and practice are further compounded when a district contracts with one of many software training companies that rely upon business examples and know little or nothing about education.

When "Office" training becomes the norm, we should not be surprised that many teachers rebel at the intrusion of office metaphors, examples and content into programs that should, instead, focus on schools, classrooms, curriculum and students. Districts should, instead, provide "School" learning experiences and opportunities.

The training model sometimes adds insult to injury by rushing the learner through dozens of skills in too short a time period with insufficient guided practice to reach a comfortable level of familiarity and skill. If the trainer rushes the learners, there is great danger that the anxiety, concern and latent resistance of many of the more reluctant learners will be aggravated.

Even after twenty years of bringing these new technologies into schools and offering training, we are finding that a large percentage of teachers reports feeling ill prepared to use them in curriculum rich ways.

Data reported in **Education Week's Technology Counts '99** shows that teachers are not making widespread use of their networks now that many more schools and classrooms are wired. They also found that most teachers reported that they were not well prepared to use new technologies.

http://www.edweek.org/sreports/tc99/tables/us-t1.htm

There is considerable risk that districts will now rush to fill the professional development void with hundreds of hours of teacher training – hours that are unlikely to convert reluctant, late adopting, skeptical teachers into true believers and frequent users.

How Teachers Learn

Main Principles of Adult Learning

What do we mean by "adult learning" and how does it differ from the training models that have dominated technology related professional development for the past two decades?

The clearest way to contrast **adult learning** (often called "**andragogy**") with **pedagogy** (instructor directed learning) is to note that adult learning usually involves the learner in activities that match that person's interests, needs, style, and developmental readiness.

Fundamental beliefs:

1) **The learner may make choices from a rich and varied menu of learning experiences and possibilities.**

2) **Learners must take responsibility for planning, acting, and growing**.

If we shift school cultures to support adult learning, professional development is experienced as **a personal journey of growth and discovery** that engages the learner on a daily and perhaps hourly basis. In the best cases, andragogy includes an emphasis upon self-direction, transformation and experience. One learns by doing and exploring . . . by trying, by failing, by changing and adapting strategies, and by overcoming obstacles after many trials.

Unlike the training models, adult learning is primarily concerned with creating the conditions, as well as the inclination and the competencies to transfer new tools and skills into daily practice. While training usually occurs outside of context and frequently ignores issues of transfer, adult learning is all about melding practice with context. Adult learning should encourage teachers to identify and then remove obstacles.

What matters is what happens back in the classroom on Monday morning.

Professional Development as Organizational Development

The most effective learning strategies require a change in the ways teachers spend their time and the ways they work together. Frequently we notice how informal support systems, partnerships, teams, and collaborative structures may be the most efficacious elements in a broad-based change effort.

As mentioned previously, gardening provides a useful metaphor for this process. We will see more growth if we cultivate the soil and fertilize before planting. An exclusive focus on skills and software is a bit like spreading seeds across a concrete playground.

While some maintain that reluctance to use new technologies is simply rooted in a lack of skill and confidence, there is evidence from Becker and Fullan that teachers need to be recruited. They must be convinced of the value of the new activities and then given ample time to work on teams to invent effective lessons.

In many schools, teachers are isolated from each other and preoccupied with what Fullan calls "the daily press" of getting through their schedule, focused according to Becker on state standards. Quite a few of these teachers are likely to cling to routines they have enjoyed in the past until they are equipped and encouraged to find, invent, and test new routines that are suitable and reliable replacements.

This creative exploration, invention, and testing will require a change in schools that breaks down isolation, facilitates the work of teams and provides ample time for program development.

The work of Michael Fullan, Bruce Joyce, Terence Deal and Ann Lieberman makes it quite clear that real change requires attention to many organizational issues rarely addressed by those installing networks and computers.

How can it be that so much school reform has taken place over the last century yet schooling appears pretty much the same as it's always been?

Larry Cuban

Effective Strategies and Projects

A. Professional Development Plans (PGPs)

The district adopts a professional growth program with the support of the teacher association that clarifies the commitment of the Board and the staff to the value of ongoing professional development and change.

A key component of such a program is the individual growth plan (PGP) written within district guidelines by each teacher and then shared with the building principal. This document becomes the road map to guide each teacher's learning during the year and helps the principal to be an effective supervisor, providing resources and support as needed.

Typically, the teacher lists 2-3 main areas for growth along with the activities most likely to promote the growth. One goal might be to acquire the technology and instructional skills to launch classroom research projects using a model such as WebQuests or Research Modules listed at http://fno.org/url.html.

If the district has made a major investment in new technologies, all teachers might be asked to include a technology integration goal.

B. **Study Groups**

Teachers gather in small groups of their own choosing to meet on a weekly basis for an hour or more to pursue shared growth goals as listed in their PGPs. They determine the best path toward completion of the goals. They may sign up for classes, call for small tutorials, browse online resources, read outstanding professional books, and attend conferences together.

In keeping with the tenets of adult learning, teachers learn best when they can make choices in content, pacing, and styles while enjoying the support of a team of like-minded fellow learners. Carlene Murphy (1998) and others have developed and tested study group models that fruitfully engage every teacher in such activities.

C. **Curriculum Development/Invention Teams**

When teams of teachers gather to build standards-based units that they can actually use with their students, some remarkable technology learning takes place. Mixing late adopting, skeptical teachers on the same team with early adopting, enthusiastic teachers and a strong school librarian leads to convergence and mutual respect as all the inventors find common ground during the invention process. http://staffdevelop.org/invent.html

Even though the focus of these activities might be student learning and curriculum, participants are "learning by doing" – another basic tenet of adult learning. Those with limited technology skills often emerge with far more comfort, skill, and competence. More importantly, they develop the appetite and inclination to use these new tools so often lacking.

Baltimore County, Maryland , Grand Prairie, Texas, and the Country Areas Program in New South Wales (Australia) have employed this invention team strategy to create dozens of research modules. http://fno.org/url.html.

The San Diego Schools involved many of its teachers in a Challenge Grant program that took three years, immersed teachers in substantial learning, and resulted in the creation of many outstanding WebQuests. The full story is well documented at http://projects.edtech.sandi.net/.

Participating schools were asked to commit matching funds and twenty per cent of the teachers. In the first summer they built a foundation of technology and curriculum planning skills. In subsequent summers, learning strategies such as the use of graphic organizers and scaffolding became the focus as they turned to the actual building of units. Examples can be found at http://projects.edtech.sandi.net/projects/.

D. Technology Coaches, Mentors and Cadres

Just as novice rock climbers and pilots benefit from the tutelage and support of more experienced climbers and fliers, schools find that teachers can make good progress with the kinds of learning associated with new technologies if they have skilled partners working alongside during the lesson development and implementation stages.

Some districts assign effective classroom teachers to this mentor and coaching role full time for a year or more so that classroom teachers have a built in support system to take them through the most difficult early stages. The mentor's involvement is temporary and planned to drop away as the novice teacher develops skill and confidence.

In a related strategy, schools create leadership cadres with a broad mix of teacher types who take the time and trouble to explore the leading edge of new practices and sort through the often inflated claims to help the rest of the teachers focus their learning on opportunities worth pursuing. The creation of such internal leadership requires a substantial investment by the district, but the return on investment is high as the district can protect itself from bandwagons and unhealthy reliance upon outside consultants and vendors.

The cadre becomes a prime aspect of planning the professional development opportunities to be offered to the rest of the staff. http://staffdevelop.org/cadre.html.

In Omaha, Nebraska, the Educational Service Unit #3 made peer coaching and the cadre a key ingredient of its highly successful grant supported project, "the Learning Web." Invention teams from surrounding school districts gather each summer to invent curriculum units with strong technology elements. Each team works with a specially trained facilitator to guide the process. http://www.esu3.org/special/institute/index.html.

E. Informal Support Groups and Support Staffing
"Just in Time Support"

Following up on the gardening metaphor mentioned earlier, each school tries to deepen the resources available on a day to day basis so that any teacher who is frustrated, blocked, or having difficulties is likely to find help within just a few minutes.

Instead of relying upon a few specialists who will never seem available, the school makes sure that one third of the staff is quite good at something and can be called upon to support colleagues who are looking for guidance, encouragement, and timely troubleshooting assistance.

Supplementing this adult support would be gender balanced support from students – what one media specialist calls her "tech tutors" – students who are taught how to support others diplomatically in their technology efforts.

In the Antelope Valley Union High School District, California, where laptop carts are an important strategy, this "just in time support" is also delivered at each of several high schools by providing extra staffing rarely available in most schools.

The AVUHSD provides the following at each of its six high schools: 1) a full time instructional technology teacher with technology coaching responsibilities (might be shared between two people in some schools), 2) a one period laptop coordinator, 3) a technology aide responsible for keeping all the laptop carts and equipment operating at full capacity, 4) one or more computer lab assistants and one or more full time network support technicians. This staffing makes just in time support a reality so teachers can focus on teaching.

http://www.avdist.org

F. Help Lines & FAQs

Just as many companies are finding that customers can get timely assistance through online help resources & FAQs, schools could and should provide many more of these kinds of support systems so that teachers can swiftly find answers to commonly asked questions and frequently encountered problems. The willingness to take technology risks may be encouraged by the availability of a friendly person on a help line to erase the sense of isolation and frustration.

G. Excursions: School and Work Place Visits, Conferences, etc.

Significant shifts in behavior and understanding can occur when teachers have a chance to see more of the outside world. Typically isolated from new developments in the workplace or in other schools, teachers have little basis for shifting their own behaviors, little opportunity to appreciate the upheaval in practices around them. A day spent behind the scenes in an architectural office, a shipping company or a newspaper can transform perspectives and prove very motivating. The whole notion of excursions has tremendous value provided the visits are followed by well structured consideration of ramifications for the learning program back at school.

H. Online Learning

Many teachers are beginning to taste a mixture of online learning experiences that allow for progress without attending formal classes as we have known them. Some of these new offerings are little more than 1950s college syllabi dressed up with online reading assignments and chat sessions. Others offer learning that is enticing, substantial, and generative.

Districts can now contract for online professional development programs with providers such as:

Apex Learning
http://www.apexlearning.com/td/
Classroom Connect's Connected University
http://cu.classroom.com/
Teacher Universe
http://teacheruniverse.com/

If designed properly, these online learning programs may offer many of the following advantages:

An emphasis on learning as opposed to teaching
Learning independent of time or place
Self-paced
Customized
Competency-based
No heroes needed
Uniform
Cost effective

For a full explanation, see "Web-Based Learning: A Strategy to Avoid Heroics." http://staffdevelop.org/online.html

Orchestration

The best approach is to blend many of the strategies above together so that they create a compounding impact on the learning culture. They may each make an important contribution separately, but broad-based change and the widespread use of new technologies will usually demand a more comprehensive effort. The strings, the woodwinds, and the percussion section cannot carry the symphony by themselves.

An effective program requires the skillful orchestration of all of these program elements to achieve the kind of synergy that leads to major transformations and shifts in practice.

Resource Issues

When a district puts the horse before the cart, investing all of its money in equipment and networking rather than taking a more balanced approach, the strategies outlined in this article may seem preposterous. These districts rarely have any money left over for human infrastructure once they have finished with the installation of a network.

But it need not be so. If districts slow down and take advantage of concepts such as "strategic deployment" – moving wireless computers around to maximize usage – they can achieve a higher amount of actual contact time with fewer desktops. Unfortunately, most districts spread the equipment out thinly and evenly so that no teachers have "critical mass." In many of these classrooms, the equipment will see little use.

For alternatives strategies, see "Picking up the Tab for Robust Professional Development" at http://staffdevelop.org/funding.html.

Before committing most funds to equipment, boards should give attention to planning concepts such as "the total cost of ownership." (Van Dam, 1999) While it may be tempting to focus on the hardware, it is a dangerous and shortsighted approach.

Measuring Return on Investment

There is far too little assessment being done to guide professional development. Most districts do not know the level of development already achieved by staff, let alone their preferences, styles, fears and passions. A thoughtful assessment strategy helps to identify offerings that stand a chance of matching preferences, and then assessment makes it possible to steer the program forward. See "Finding Your Way Through The Data Smog" by Joe Slowinski at http://fno.org/sept00/data.html.

The Bottom Line

We expect to see daily, effective use of new technologies in standards-based, curriculum rich lessons. We should be able to walk down the hallways of any school in the district and note teachers and students using tools in appropriate, powerful ways . . . sometimes a book, sometimes a calculator, sometimes a networked computer.

If we invest in robust professional development with an emphasis upon adult learning strategies, we expect all teachers to learn, to grow and to move forward, sometimes relying on high touch, sometimes on high tech, sometimes with a magical blend of both.

Four teachers and two administrators have flown two thousand miles to attend a national conference on educational uses of new information technologies. They boarded the plane confident that they would return home armed with research findings to guide decision-making. They are united in their faith that decisions should be guided by data.

- What works?
- What fails?
- How can we do our best by the students?
- How do we get the optimal return on our technology investments?

Sadly, they are disillusioned by the lack of significant research being conducted by most educational communities rushing to network schools.

"There's a big gap here," complains Sally, the veteran technology enthusiast of the team. So committed is she to the vision that she is spending evenings, weekends, and summers picking up an advanced degree in educational technology. "There is so little research to help us think about our choices."

The team is camped out in an espresso Internet cafe several blocks from the Convention Center. It is the final morning of the final day, and they are having trouble mobilizing for the closing keynote.

"I'm tired of all these promises and visions and the whole 'new new thing,'" adds Gregory, the team's hardened skeptic. "I haven't found a single session where they reported sound research."

At this point, one of the administrators joins in. "Well, I did find one session - the one by Hank Becker from UCI - and his reports are a good start, but I agree that there were slim pickings, unless, of course, we include the corporation funded reports."

"I tried a few of those," laughed Sally, "and they failed to meet any of the research design standards I am expected to observe in my graduate classes. They were quite biased. Seems like we're going home empty-handed."

The Research Gap

Answering Key Questions

Educational research is meant to help us to explore the most important questions we have at the end of each day. In the best of worlds, research would also provide guidance for educators to make wise choices from the sometimes bewildering menu being thrust toward them by eager vendors.

Providing Guidance

Given dozens of ways to use laptops or desktop computers once they arrive in our classrooms, which uses are most productive and which professional development experiences are needed to bring about the most return on investment?

If a district hoped to improve student scores on a demanding state writing test, for example, planners would want to know which of the following would have the greatest payoffs . . .

Six Writing Strategies

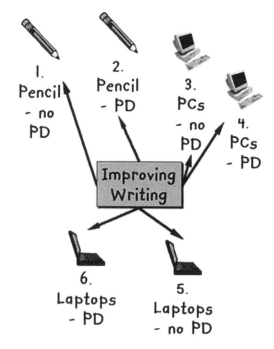

Strategy 1 - Frequent guided writing practice with pencil, paper, and no special strategy.

Strategy 2 - Frequent guided writing practice with pencil, paper and an emphasis upon "writing as process" supported by cluster diagramming and the use of the Six Traits approach to writing. (Culham and Spandel) Teachers spend two weeks in the summer in writers workshops learning how to do "writing as process" with the Six Traits approach.

Strategy 3 - Frequent guided writing practice with 10 hours of weekly computer time for each student using desktop computers, and no special strategy.

Strategy 4 - Frequent guided writing practice with 10 hours of weekly computer time for each student using desktop computers and an emphasis upon "writing as process" supported by cluster diagramming using the Inspiration™ software program and the Six Traits approach to writing. Teachers spend two weeks in the summer in writers workshops learning how to do "writing as process" as well as the Six Traits approach.

Strategy 5 - Frequent guided writing practice with students having their own laptop computers and no special strategy.

Strategy 6 - Frequent guided writing practice with students having their own laptop computers and an emphasis upon "writing as process" supported by cluster diagramming using the Inspiration software program and the Six Traits approach to writing. Teachers spend two weeks in the summer in writers workshops learning how to do "writing as process" and use Inspiration ™ plus the Six Traits approach on their own laptop computers.

A properly designed study of these six strategies would prove enlightening, but no credible, comprehensive, comparative studies exist on writing or any other major educational question related to the impact of new technologies.

Reliability Issues

The design of reliable educational research is beyond the scope of this article, but there are classic books, like Campbell and Stanley **Experimental and Quasi-Experimental Designs for Research** (1966, Houghton Mifflin College; ISBN: 0395307872) that outline the traits of a credible study. Unfortunately, many of the reports gaining national attention these days do not meet those specifications.

A recent example would be an Educational Testing Service study, "Does it Compute? The Relationship Between Educational

The Research Gap

Technology and Student Achievement in Mathematics," by Harold Wenglinsky, exploring relationships between computer experiences and math performance on the NAEP tests (National Assessment of Educational Progress.) http://www.ets.org/research/pic/technolog.html.

This study found that certain teacher strategies were associated with lower math performance while others were associated with higher performance (but only at some grade levels.)

The researchers did what is called *ex post facto* research. Rather than setting up a study to test hypotheses with all confounding conditions controlled, they take data from a broader study and "mine" the data to find links between various events.

This kind of research shows association but does not show cause. We can see a correlation between phone ownership in African countries and lower infant mortality, but that doesn't mean we could reduce infant mortality by purchasing more phones for everybody.

Phone ownership is an indicator of wealth. Wealthy countries have better inoculation programs, better nutrition, and better water quality — some likely causes of lower infant mortality. Using *ex post facto* research we could (erroneously) claim that people should buy more phones to save children's lives!

Objectivity Issues

A standard issue in research is the possibility that researchers might have a vested interest in the outcome of the study. Validity and credibility is undermined when the authors and funders are closely allied and likely to benefit if the study comes out in a manner that makes their product look good. This basic rule is frequently ignored today as companies pay for research without observing the objectivity standards and are then able to win national press attention by virtue of their superior public relations resources while more credible academic research fails to gain notice.

Theory Testing

What we need is more theory testing like the writing example provided earlier. Schools need well constructed, publicly funded, academically sound research to determine which strategies are most likely to produce the learning outcomes required to meet performance and curriculum goals. Instead, we are seeing an increase in national reports attempting to describe what is happening across the land.

The Research Gap

Before a public opinion pollster can claim to describe behaviors and attitudes of the general public, they must discuss how their sample is representative. Most of the recent reports have failed to meet that standard, but are still quick to make generalizations. Their findings about teachers use of the Internet may be based on one district employee's speculation, for example.

The New York Cybertimes of December 1, 1999 summarizes a report, "Technology in Education 1999," a Market Data Retrieval report about computers in the schools. One finding . . .

"And 54 percent of schools report that a majority of their teachers are now using the Internet in instruction."

This conclusion contrasts dramatically with previous reports by Becker and others that show much smaller percentages of use by teachers in instruction.

> . . . a minority of teachers had students use Web browsers during the last school year (36%) . . .
> Becker, "Internet Use by Teachers," p. 6,
> http://www.crito.uci.edu/TLC/FINDINGS/internet-use/
> startpage.htm

> What might be called "regular" use — using the World Wide Web to do research on at least 10 occasions — was a practice of nearly one-quarter of all teachers with a modem in their classrooms and 30% of those with direct high-speed connections."
> Becker, p. 6

The reporter does an excellent job of adding interviews from skeptics who raise the point that the type of use is more important than the amount of access, but the 54% statistic stands unchallenged, even though it is highly speculative in its origins, being based on self reports of schools and teachers with sample sizes often quite limited and possibly skewed.

In one Market Data Retrieval report for **Technology Counts'99**, for example, the responses were quite low . . .

> On April 28, surveys were mailed to a stratified sample of 15,000 teachers—classroom teachers at the elementary school level and English, mathematics, science, and social studies teachers at the middle and high school levels. 1,407 teachers

responded by the cutoff date of May 21.

http://www.schooldata.com/publications3.html

An educational researcher would be expected to comment on how respondents might differ from non-respondents, but Market Data Retrieval remains silent on this important issue.

What Research is Needed

We need much more research comparing learning strategies for both teachers and students. We see little that would help us to make choices. So far the research on teachers has done little but count the hours of training. There is little differentiating between software training courses and adult learning strategies such as study groups and mentor programs. They all are lumped together.

We also need to know more about the consequences of different delivery systems and types of equipment deployment. Are we better off spreading computers evenly across all classrooms, for example, than moving them about in strategic clusters? Most important of all, we need government funding for robust, independent research that will free schools from reliance upon research driven by marketing concerns and interests.

Chapter 14 - Beyond Edutainment and Technotainment

Urban and perpetually under-funded through the final decades of the last century, the Middle School of the Future (previously named the Booker T. Washington Middle School) has dramatically closed the "digital divide" facing many urban schools today thanks to generous sponsorships, contributions and partnerships from technologically committed corporate friends.

For this school plagued by poor performance, illiteracy, and low attendance during the 1990s, the principal has banked heavily on the possibilities of notebook computers and networked information. She is hoping to reverse the old patterns, equipping students with all the skills and competencies they might need to break into successful futures.

Sharon Jackson is a veteran principal with 30 years of doing the impossible. Every school she has touched has changed for the better. She has led with passionate beliefs. She has made students feel prized. She has created hope and progress whenever she has led a school.

Never quite satisfied with her most recent efforts, Sharon has kept her eyes open for new resources, strategies, and tools to lift student performance to higher levels. Not so long ago, when Sharon attended a national conference devoted to the promise of networks and notebook computers, she found herself swayed by the testimonials of other educators .

She watched a series of PowerPoint™ presentations with slides promising major changes:

Laptops make a change in classrooms . . .
- Lessons change
- Activities change
- Student attitudes change
- Classroom management changes
- Assessment changes

Beyond Edutainment

She liked much of what she heard and read, but she was also troubled by some examples of student work held up as evidence of great success.

The three-day conference was structured around dozens of Power-Point™ presentations. Some of these slide shows came from fellow educators outlining the ingredients of a successful program. Others were student-produced.

As Sharon sat through the presentations, she was struck by the thin quality of the student work, with an emphasis upon flash and special effects rather than content and thought.

She had sat through too many flying letters, animations and sound effects without seeing much original thought or analysis. In most cases, the medium had shoved the message aside. Intent on producing students with strong reading, writing, and thinking skills, she shook her head at the razzle-dazzle being promoted.

As she sat watching these presentations, Sharon remembered reading Jane Healy's critique of these school technology uses in **Failure to Connect** (1998).

Even as she determined to pursue her dream of a school rich with digital resources, she realized that the path might be lined with temptations, distractions, and elements of risk that the conference had failed to address.

Sharon had no intention of introducing her school to a new kind of illiteracy - an electronic version. Her prime goal was showing students how to make sense of their worlds, preparing them to think and read deeply and well. Her purpose was literacy - not illiteracy or e-literacy.

She had little interest in the flashy, the glib, or the superficial. She was no fan of edutainment or technotainment. She was clear about her purpose.

Even as she moved forward with plans for a school well equipped with notebook computers, Sharon kept her focus on teaching, learning, and thinking. To her, the equipment was nothing much more than a set of new tools to support questioning, exploring and creating. She fully expected that her students would make great gains on the tests recently introduced and causing panic across her state.

While schools consider the vast array of new electronic tools and resources made available by eager vendors and publishers, some teachers and school leaders are awakening to the challenge of resisting the glib, the superficial and the disneyfied aspects of the digital economy and society. In some cases, it seems as if installation and purchase precede purpose, but in others, a strong sense of educational philosophy helps schools sail past the shallow waters and the navigational hazards of this brave new electronic world.

This chapter identifies the risks of edutainment and technotainment while suggesting strategies to optimize return on technology investments as measured by gains in student performance.

Shallow Waters

Schools can ill afford technotainment activities during a time of tough new standards and tests. We might define technotainment as technology activities heavily laced with entertainment but essentially lacking in rigor or value.

Technotainment often stresses technology for technology's sake without enhancing student reading, writing, and reasoning skills.

"What did you do in school today?"

"The Internet."

Such answers might mean anything from surfing pop culture sites to serious reading of periodical articles, but it often seems enough that students are using networked computers in some way — any way! Technology becomes a goal in itself.

To determine whether an activity falls under the category of technotainment, apply the chart on the next page to the lesson.

As tests shift to require inferential reasoning and problem solving, the focus of teachers and schools must be on strategic reading and thinking across the disciplines. In Ohio, for example, eighth graders read a long passage about a new piano in Annie's home. The story describes Annie waiting while her brother lectures her.

After answering a series of multiple choice questions, they are asked to write an extended answer to the following question:

Some stories emphasize plot, or what happens. Others stress character, using action and speech to reveal what characters are like. Tell which you think this story stresses — plot or character. Tell whether you think it does so successfully. Support your answer with references from the story.

Traits of Technotainment

Trait	Y/N
1. Pointless The activity involves the use of a tool such as a spreadsheet or presentation program without an authentic connection to the regular (social studies, science, etc.) curriculum for the grade level of the student. PowerPointing and spreadsheeting become goals rather than just means to ends.	
2. Unstandard The activity is disconnected from state standards and the new tests. No relationship or contribution made to the students' grasp of either content or skills.	
3. Robotic The activity requires little original thought or higher level thinking. The student blindly follows directions and wins success by taking orders.	
4. Glib The activity requires nothing more than skimming along the surface of the content without probing, exploring, asking essential questions, or creating new insight.	
5. Static The activity does nothing to advance the skill level or the skill repertoire of the student. Same old, same old!	
6. Disneyfied The activity is sugar coated and packaged with arcade quality graphics as if learning must be turned into a game or cartoon before young people will find it rewarding.	
7. Flashy Special effects, transitions, bells, and whistles are prevalent. Students are encouraged to devote more than 25% of their time and effort to packaging and special effects rather than the thought, the content, and the production of new ideas.	
8. Empty The activity does little to advance student understanding of any issue, question, or idea worth study.	

Beyond Edutainment

To lift the performance of students on such challenging items, teachers must provide each student with a skill repertoire such as the one outlined in "Scoring High with New Technologies" at http://fno.org/apr99/covapr.html

- Questioning
- Picturing
- Awakening prior knowledge
- Synthesis
- Inferring
- Fluency

Gaining full competency with these skills then will require frequent and repeated practice on challenges similar to the items students will encounter on state tests as outlined in "Teaching to the Standards" at http://fno.org/nov99/standards.html

We are learning that it is not enough to wire schools or place networked computers in classrooms. We must make wise choices that focus on student outcomes worth achieving, upon value added rather than glitz, glimmer and gimmicks. We are moving past edutainment and technotainment to a new form of literacy combining the best of the old with the best of the new.

Strategic Deployment of Hardware to Maximize Readiness, Staff Use, and Student Achievement

As schools install networks, planners must pay more attention to the strategic pacing and placement of equipment. Wise decision-makers will slow down long enough to prepare the way before spreading equipment far and wide. They will devote themselves to readiness.

While it may please hardware and software companies to fill classrooms with computers before teachers are prepared or inclined to use them with frequency and good intentions, it is bad policy and worse economics.

We have been spending too much money on infrastructure and equipment . . . too little on readiness.

When combined with robust professional development, the strategic pacing and placement of equipment keep the technology "cart" where it belongs. Wise schools put program first. Equipment follows. No computer before its time. No room before its time. No teachers before they are ready.

Readiness is paramount.

Strategic pacing and placement optimize the impact of our technology investments on student learning, giving us the maximum return on our dollars, reaching the largest possible number of students while minimizing "down time."

Strategic Pacing

Strategic pacing is the thoughtful timing of computer purchase and installation to coincide with staff readiness.

It is tempting to buy enough computers to spread them out

through all the classrooms the moment the network is installed, but it makes far better sense for most schools to phase the equipment into the building over a 2-3 year time period. The computers move about where they will do the most good.

We avoid the "dilution trap" - the well intentioned strategy of spreading resources thinly but equally across all classrooms in the name of fairness - a decision which actually means that no teacher and no classroom will attain "critical mass."

No computer or classroom before its (it's) time!

Most faculties are made up of a spectrum of teachers ranging from "early adopters" to "late adopters." The early adopters (usually about 25% of a typical staff) are ready and eager to make dramatic use of networked resources. Late adopters (who often account for 40-60% of a typical staff) are quite skeptical, reluctant, and resistant. If you place networked computers in late adopters' rooms before they have been successfully recruited and prepared, there is little chance the computers will be used.

Between the early and late adopters is a group of teachers who might welcome new technologies if someone would just show them how and why they belong in a science, math, or social studies classroom. They want to see lesson plans and evidence that these new tools will help them to address increasingly demanding state standards and tests. They have many urgent questions about practical classroom management issues. They expect answers.

Strategic pacing puts the first wave of equipment into the classrooms and programs of early adopters who will make immediately fruitful use of the hardware to support student learning. Succeeding waves enter classrooms as less enthusiastic (and less prepared) staff members acquire the skills, the readiness, the inclination, and the unit plans to make full use of information technologies. Classroom access to networked computers is "won" over time by teachers who commit to a personal journey of growth. Districts may also speed this process through a mixture of incentives and clearly stated performance expectations.

Clarifying Curriculum Expectations Before Installation

Under the principle of "no program or classroom before its time," we expect to see well articulated curriculum plans for how this information technology will enhance the reading, writing, reasoning and research of students in each discipline. These expectations should be published before the broad-based distribution of equipment across classrooms, but curriculum guides are frequently silent regarding the use of the network. First the equipment arrives, and then teachers are left to their own devices.

Invention teams composed of both early and late adopters should be convened in the summer before network installation to create lesson plans and unit plans that hold great promise for promoting student achievement. Such teams may build upon models such as **WebQuests** (http://edweb.sdsu.edu/webquest/webquest.html) or **Research Modules** (http://fno.org/module/module4.html).

While the two primary benefits of new information technologies are support for student research and student communication, few schools have made a formal curriculum commitment to either continuous student research or to collaborative e-mail projects.

Unfortunately, concerned about safety and violence issues, many schools are blocking student use and access even as the new equipment is installed, adding barriers to the full use of the network before the staff has even considered how the resources might enhance student learning. Chapter 16 describes three ways that schools are blocking student use of networks.

Beyond Techology (McKenzie, 2000) outlined strategies to improve the reading, writing, and reasoning of students. If schools would adopt and adapt such program strategies as part of each curriculum area, teachers would be less skeptical and more enthusiastic about the new equipment.

Strategic Placement

We see far too little consideration of movement. The prevailing strategy is to install and lock down all new computers. Yet this strategy is incredibly wasteful and inefficient.

Strategic Placement involves a marriage of equipment and program. When the biology teacher is ready to launch a major study of the rain forest, we wheel a dozen networked computers into the classroom - enough resources to support genuine program integration.

Strategic Placement takes us past tokenism and lip service to authentic engaged learning activities.

Most elementary teachers require 6-8 computers (critical mass) to support a technologically meaningful program.

Secondary teachers may need 10-15. The only way to achieve

these numbers is to move computers around or to create small labs which students can visit. Unfortunately, many systems departments resist movement of equipment. Even though many schools have experienced success with COWS (Computers on Wheels), the strategy has been virtually suppressed.

Moving computers where they are needed and wanted allows a school to cut its hardware budget in half while slowing down the purchasing and replacement cycle. Instead of installing 2-3 computers per classroom that will be used (maybe) 15% of the time, the district cuts its order for 2000 computers down to 1000, invests heavily in professional development and realizes 85% utilization by moving the equipment to where it will be welcomed (and used).

One week here. One week there. Movement spawns use!

This is a remarkably simple and obvious strategy, infused with common sense and grounded in what we know about change in schools. Why, then, have we heard so little about this approach?

Unfortunately, much of the media and much of the planning information available to schools is paid for or subsidized by companies whose profits would be sorely undercut by such restraint.

These same companies are pushing for laptop schools and computers in every classroom even though we have no credible evidence that this is a wise investment.

Networked computers currently become obsolete within 30-36 months of purchase because of the way the network and systems software companies keep "enhancing" their programs.

Currently popular schemes for networking schools are surprisingly ungrounded in learning theory or sound educational practice. Placing 2-3 computers (or even 4-5 computers) in every classroom regardless of staff readiness is a bit like pouring seeds on a playground and expecting a meadow to sprout.

Just a few decades back we were told that we could revolutionize schooling by placing a TV monitor in the corner of every classroom. This TV would offer students amazing teachers (instead of normal ones) and education would be changed forever.

Schools jumped on the instructional TV bandwagon back then, full of hope and expectation, only to discover that TV is a cold medium that can never quite inspire great learning.

Some of the same folks are back with this latest technology initiative making bold promises. Sometimes they call it "distance learning." But the most important problem is their lack of understanding of learning, learning theories, children, classrooms, and instruction.

Strategic Deployment

Return on Investment

What schools should consider is the learning that results from various strategies, weighing the costs and benefits of each when making design choices. Unfortunately, the prime consideration, as mentioned in Chapter 2, can be network efficiency rather than student learning.

When networking becomes the primary goal, decisions are often made that may diminish the return on investment with regard to student performance. Without an assessment program that might show there has been little impact on classrooms, the equipping of a district can proceed with little accountability. In many cases, "ignorance is bliss."

Chapter 16 - Waste Not, Want Not

It makes no sense to spend the millions of dollars required to network a school district and then drastically curtail student use of the network to placate runaway adult fears.

In many places, the rush to network schools is a scandal waiting to be discovered and reported. The failure to provide adequate professional development as well as sufficient technical support results in what previous chapters have called "The Screensavers Disease" as millions of computers sit unused or poorly used throughout major portions of the school day and night. This chapter explores a related failure of leadership and resolve that has worsened already disappointing levels of utilization.

Billions of dollars are being wasted by schools and districts that undermine the value of newly installed networks by adopting anxiety-driven policies that minimize student use of the networks. They install a daunting array of governors, training wheels, filters, brakes, and other encumbrances which reduce the benefits of their already struggling programs to a dismal trickle.

Warning Signs

1. Students are denied access to e-mail privileges or are given only temporary privileges for special heavily supervised projects.

2. Students are denied access to information on topics such as "breast cancer" because "breast" is considered a "dirty word" and the schools have installed filters on networks which block legitimate information along with undesirable and controversial sources.

3. Students are denied access to electronic storage on the district network so they cannot collect and save the information and graphics they discover while researching. They cannot build up project files on the network or share such files with partners.

Waste Not, Want Not

In the best of situations, networks serve at least two important educational purposes:

A. Global Communications - Robust networks connect students to a global community of learners, scholars and citizens through e-mail that supports communication - the exchange of ideas across state and national boundary lines. Progressive, democratic countries report the rapid growth of e-mail communication as a basic tool of citizenship while repressive countries outlaw the ownership of modems and try to limit access to e-mail. Many corporations routinely expect employees to solve problems on geographically remote teams united only by e-mail and networks.

If schools are meant to prepare students for citizenship and employment in an Age of Information, they must not withhold this basic communication tool.

B. Information Literacy - Robust networks connect students to a vast network of valuable data sources, some of which come free over the Internet and some of which must be purchased. Instead of limiting students to heavily filtered and condensed versions of the world such as textbooks, networks (along with good print libraries) allow students to develop their own views and independent problem-solving abilities. The value of such access depends heavily upon the provision of substantial training in the component skills associated with information literacy.

Sadly, many school districts act swiftly to minimize the benefits of their networks. It is as if the mere connecting of classrooms to a global network is the end purpose of the project.

We are finally wired. We have a computer in each classroom tied to the Internet.

- Display device? No.
- Student e-mail? No.
- Internet browser? No.
- Professional development? Next year.
- Technicians? One for our 1,000 computers.
- Staff and student storage on network? No.

Waste Not, Want Not

The Issue of Student Access to E-Mail

Because there are no reliable statistics defining the risk to children posed by e-mail, the sensationalist coverage of this issue by some members of the press has created unreasonable fears. These fears have led to severe restrictions on the use of e-mail by students in many school districts.

When **From Now On** polled five Washington state school districts that installed networks and allowed student e-mail starting in 1995, all five reported that they still offer e-mail to students in 1999 and could report no kidnappings, attacks, stalkings or sexual abuse attributable to student use of e-mail. Instead of problems and disasters, these same districts claimed important educational benefits had resulted from their provision of student e-mail (see table on the page 125).

Unfortunately, an occasional tragedy reported far and wide by the news services is often blown into a *cause celebre*. Overly cautious school administrators and board members sometimes translate these news stories into policies and procedures that restrict students to occasional glimpses of the electronic highway from the cyber-equivalent of overpasses and distant hilltops.

These overblown and exaggerated tales of e-mail danger do the present generation of children a great disservice. Even though children have faced risks walking to and from school for many decades, no one has seriously suggested that student walking be outlawed.

During most of this century, responsible school administrators and teachers have equipped elementary students with neighborhood survival skills. They learn how to avoid strangers. They do not accept candy or climb into strangers' cars even when these strangers offer convincing stories about an accident to one's mother or father. They learn safe telephone behavior when they are home alone. Schools have quite successfully taught children the wise use of technologies long before the Internet.

Why the sudden big fuss about e-mail?

During the six years I was an elementary principal in New Jersey during the 1970s and early 1980s, not a single year passed without at least one scare related to strangers in cars bothering young children walking home from school. One year a child was murdered on the way to school. (The killer turned out to be the child's own distraught parent.)

In another district I went through the devastating process of removing a very popular teacher from a classroom as a result of allegations (later proven true) that this teacher was a sexual offender.

Waste Not, Want Not

These real time threats to children predated the Internet but continue to be far more prevalent risks for children in most towns than those posed by e-mail, provided the school introduces e-mail in a responsible manner.

The easy path is to limit or prohibit student access to e-mail. Another associated strategy is to "wash one's hands" of responsibility and let students use one of the free e-mail programs currently available. But both of these approaches abdicate a fundamental responsibility to prepare students for citizenship in the next century.

If schools leave e-mail education to non-educators, we miss an opportunity to teach ethical and responsible behavior. Even worse, we deepen the already severe gap between those with home computers and those without. The table on page 127 suggests strategies to engage students in the use of e-mail in ways that are safe and responsible.

Examples of Excellent E-Mail Projects

Judi Harris from the University of Texas at Austin has identified and collected at one site more than 300 valuable e-mail projects well suited for many of the curriculum goals teachers need to address.
http://ccwf.cc.utexas.edu/~jbharris/Virtual-Architecture/Telecollaboration/more-telecollaboration.html

Also, Tammy Payton of Loogootee Community Schools has compiled an excellent list of online projects your class may join.
http://www.siec.k12.in.us/~west/online/join.htm

Censorship is Censorship is Censorship

If it walks like a duck, squawks like a duck, swims like a duck, flies like a duck and lays eggs like a duck . . . chances are quite good that it is a duck.
Ancient Chinese Proverb

Currently masquerading under the pseudonyms "filtering" and "child protection" is an ominous movement to severely restrict the access of young people to all kinds of perfectly respectable and legitimate information. While the proponents of these software strategies sugar coat their restrictions by focussing most of their advertising on sexual dangers, Internet predators, and pornography, the actual impact of their filtering may extend quite far beyond these content areas.

Filtering out Internet sites with artificial intelligence is censorship,

Educational Benefits of E-Mail Reported by Early Adopting Districts	Number Reporting
1. Students contacted experts to obtain information.	5
2. Students exchanged information with students in other countries or worked on joint projects to develop some kind of product.	5
3. Students exchanged information with students in other states or worked on joint projects to develop some kind of product.	5
4. Students exchanged information with students in other schools within their state or town or worked on joint projects to develop some kind of product.	5
5. Students used e-mail with students in their own class to share findings and organize the work flow of a project.	5
6. Students used e-mail to communicate back and forth with classroom teachers about assignments and work flow for projects.	5
7. Students used e-mail and/or an internal listserv to explore and debate class associated topics.	5
8. Students used e-mail to communicate about important school issues being raised by the Student Council, the student newspaper and other student organizations.	3
9. Students used e-mail to explore with their friends various ideas, thoughts, fears and hopes typical of young people (college plans, career plans, difficulties at home, dating issues, fashion issues, good news, bad news, medical challenges, etc.)	3

plain and simple. Someone working in a corporate office or school office wipes out whole categories of information that might contain "objectionable" material. Words like "sex" and "breast" are often used as a basis for exclusion, thereby blocking students from important sources.

What makes this even worse is the failure of some products to do a decent job of excluding their alleged targets. I once tested an industry leading product and found that 30 per cent of the pornography sites encountered when searching for Pamela Anderson went unblocked. I was astounded by the false security created by the company's promises.

Reasonable Exclusion:

While school libraries and curriculum committees have always (appropriately) exercised care to weed out offensive materials before they are purchased, especially for younger children, they have also tempered those choices with discretion, acting case-by-case and title-by-title with a profound respect from the broad tastes which must coexist within a community, recognizing that libraries must serve a range of family belief systems. Controversial materials are not banned automatically from schools just to keep the peace with a minority viewpoint. While Hitler's **Mein Kampf** is objectionable, we would expect young people to have access to it.

Intellectually Bankrupt Exclusion:

In the past, school libraries have never eliminated thousands of titles based upon simplistic and intellectually bankrupt strategies like those which block all sites containing the word "breast." Few reasonable people would ever support the elimination of all books from our collections that employ the word "sex" but some of these same people will allow a corporation far away in some distant city to do just that with the Internet. It is no mere slip that many of these filtering programs often rely upon crude "artificial intelligence" to guide their exclusionary efforts.

Surrender to Narrow, Aggressive, Highly Organized Groups:

Careful selection is never quite enough to satisfy some folks, who still launch major challenges to various novels and books in our schools that they deem offensive.

In a democratic society, informational strong-arming is intolerable.

These book challenges often prove corrosive and divisive as interest groups line up on either side of a particular title. It is not enough for them to protect their own children from these experiences. They also hope to block all other children from reading this material regardless of their conflicting family values. This approach is the moral equivalent of "one size fits all" - as one group dictates what others will read and know.

Elements of Responsible E-Mail Program

1. Students are given substantial training in Internet safety before gaining access to e-mail.
2. Students are taught about ethical and responsible use of e-mail before gaining access and they are acquainted with consequences for misuse of the privilege.
3. Parents are provided classes by the school to help them guide their children's use of e-mail and the Internet. These classes include a focus on ways to monitor safe use of the Internet.
4. Parents are asked to sign a permission form indicating that they will share responsibility for their children's ethical and responsible use of e-mail.
5. Students are asked to sign the same form making a commitment to ethical and responsible use of e-mail.
6. Administrators and teachers model appropriate use of e-mail as a tool for communicating about school and curriculum.
7. Administrators and teachers firmly enforce reasonable standards for e-mail behavior from the very beginning to establish a "no-nonsense" culture.
8. Monitoring of student e-mail is conducted within school district policy guidelines which parallel other disciplinary issues such as locker searches with due and proper respect for individual rights.
9. Teachers show students how to employ e-mail as a research tool in ways that respect Netiquette and the work pressures of potential correspondents.
10. Teachers assign investigations, research projects and classroom tasks using e-mail messages to class members. They also expect students to conduct work with other class members using e-mail. They ask that finished products be submitted as electronic attachments to e-mail.
11. Teachers encourage students to enhance the school community by utilizing e-mail to exchange ideas and proposals.

This is why the American Library Association makes a strong case in its "Bill of Rights" that these decisions are family matters.

Waste Not, Want Not

The Primacy of Family Values: The best way to protect young people from offensive media - whether it be on the Internet, the television, the coffee table, or the grocery store checkout magazine display - is family values and guidance. Schools share responsibility for outlining responsible behavior on the Internet. They must enforce those expectations just as they act with regard to other disciplinary challenges. Just as we punish students for stealing lunch money or scrawling graffiti on the halls, we discipline them for displaying or printing offensive materials as outlined in our Internet policy.

The Issue of Storage on the Network

There is far too much information today, and yet there is also little consideration about how to store it electronically. Storage on the network is essential if students are going to harvest, produce, and publish.

Would you buy a car without a gas tank? Unlikely.

A chess set without a board? No way!

The wired classroom requires storage. Students spend hundreds of hours gathering and then synthesizing information - a process which demands an electronic playground for the mind. Printing out results on paper severely restricts and reduces the benefits of electronic research. Storage on the network is required to reap the benefits of the new technologies.

Think about research as a giant jigsaw puzzle with thousands (if not hundreds of thousands) of pieces which are collected and then moved about on a table top. Imagine if they made us try such a puzzle without the table!

Providing storage for students and staff is not difficult given the network software currently available and the low cost of hard drive capacity. Why is it, then, that so few districts provide storage on the district or school network as a basic way of doing business?

Sometimes the answer is simple. If the folks who design the network do not see how storage influences the educational outcomes and learning experiences of the students, they might fail to buy enough storage space even if it is cheap. Then, when asked about storage, they will (rightly) say, "It can't be done. We don't have room on the file server."

Another leading explanation is a lack of experience with the creation of teacher and student storage areas using the automated system software program. Not knowing how easy it is to create student accounts and storage, the network people might say, "It can't be done. We don't have the clerical help to set up all those accounts."

A third explanation is the fear of student abuse. "What if they start storing pornography or huge games on the network? What if we catch a virus? We don't have time to keep an eye on all of those risks."

Once again, it turns out that much of this concern can be addressed by software programs that routinely browse through storage areas looking for certain types and sizes of files. The offending student rarely escapes such searches and is soon treated to an appropriate disciplinary consequence.

Most of the excuses made and the explanations given do not hold up to scrutiny. Failing to provide storage is a bit like forgetting to fill the tank with gas, forgetting to put air in the tires, or leaving tires off the car entirely.

Most school districts are still launching their initial networking efforts. They are looking at incredibly expensive commitments and investments which might conflict with other needs such as roofs, art programs, library programs, and other essentials.

Even though this book has argued that networked schools and new technologies might improve the reading, writing, and reasoning performance of students, these improvements will be undercut if schools, administrators, and districts act to choke off the benefits of their networks by restricting access in the ways outlined in this article. It would almost be better if they saved their money and installed no network at all. Networks should not be token gestures toward modernity. They are not decoration. They are meant to be used rigorously and openly.

Chapter 17 - Pacing Change

Slow down, you move too fast.
You got to make the morning last.
Paul Simon

When it comes to networking schools and classrooms, leaders tend to rush things.

Just as folk wisdom argues that "Haste makes waste," research on change in schools warns against riding change mobiles through avalanche territory (Fullan, 1991).

Even though the shortest distance is usually a straight line, most road and railway builders know better than to head straight up a mountain without providing plenty of curves. They rely on switchbacks to keep the angle of ascent reasonable. They know engines have their limits.

Schools should follow this example. They should make the strategic pacing of change a priority if they hope to see a real (and beneficial) shift in classroom practice

Switchbacks

Schools should provide switchbacks, rest stops and plateaus as they network. They should also allow for different starting times.

unwired ------- wired ------- wireless

In the past few years we have asked teachers and students to leave behind the security of unwired classrooms in order to enjoy wired classrooms and global networks. And now we are asking them to adjust once again - this time to wireless classrooms! All the while, new state standards and tests provide a constant backdrop of storm clouds and thunder that make it hard for teachers to take risks or to embrace new strategies (Becker, 1999).

A frenzied pace of change can prove disheartening and disabling. It may create the appearance of change without any value being added. It might even stall growth as members of the community cling to the familiar in the face of threats and chaos.

A single coyote kicks up a cloud of dust digging for a long lost rabbit bone. From far away, the cloud creates the appearance of a speeding roadrunner as the wind sweeps dust along the highway.

Sometimes schools create the mere appearance of movement. But careful planning can provide the calm, the shelter, the resources and the time so teachers will make substantial, lasting progress.

Virtual change is a publicity stunt. Real change is harder to realize but infinitely more valuable.

Traits of Managed Change

1. Professional development precedes or accompanies installation. Sprinkling computers across classrooms is easy. Fostering daily, routine and robust use tied to curriculum standards is quite another matter. Districts should provide standards-based professional development that show teachers how to change student performance.

2. Program development precedes or accompanies installation. Networked computers are great for exploration and investigations, for problem-solving and engaged learning - activities that could pay off handsomely on demanding state tests and standards if the teachers are shown the connection between research, inferential reasoning, and the state standards..

3. Resources are moved about strategically where they are most welcome. Wireless computers allow rapid movement of computers where they are most welcome and will do the most good. Teachers require "critical mass" to make profitable, intense, daily use of networked computers. In most cases, they are better off with fifteen computers for one week every two months than two or three computers all year.

4. No classroom or program before its time! Premature installation creates few converts and fails to promote robust use. First we design learning experiences worth doing. Then we provide the equipment. No carts before the horses!

5. Different schedules and pathways for different folks. We make it clear that all will take the journey, but we provide latitude and choice when it comes to the timing and the nature of each professional journey of change. A sense of choice is directly associated with buy in and full participation. When teachers can match learning to their individual styles and preferences, they are more apt to travel from the tried and true.

6. Recruitment and courtship precede assignment. We will not see robust use unless we have taken the time to demonstrate the worth of the new tools and have convinced teachers that new technologies can make a real contribution. Announcing change without courtship often results in resistance rather than progress.

7. Escape is eliminated. We set a reasonable time limit, provide generous support to learn new strategies, build clear expectations into curriculum guides, and hold all teachers accountable to offer what the guides prescribe. We remove barriers, eliminate excuses, and make the new opportunities enticing.

8. Leaders question and listen. Those in charge of the implementation ask lots of questions and take the time to listen to those who must make the program work. "How is it going? How can I help? What needs changing?"

9. Retreat, regrouping, and rethinking are honored. Not everything will go as planned. Smart schools learn as they go, adjusting the plan and modifying strategies to optimize results.

Managing Quandaries, Dilemmas and Conundrums

This chapter identifies a dozen **quandaries***, **dilemmas** and **conundrums*** facing those who are intent upon introducing networked information technologies to schools. *defined on next page

There are many difficult decisions to make. And the menu overflows with conflicting values and confounding possibilities. We must chart a course between a rock and a hard place. We must steer between the devil and the deep blue sea!

Keeping up with the Joneses 1

Would we be the first in the neighborhood? The first to enjoy (and display) the coveted new glowing box which every family knew promised us liberation . . . perhaps more than liberation . . . salvation?

Would our TV be the first on the block?

> Fragment of newsprint found
> in apocryphal suburban
> Connecticut archeological
> dig site a thousand years from 1952.

This chapter can provide few definitive answers because answers and solutions must be custom-fitted to match local conditions, but the reader will find here many critically important questions that are too often overlooked in the rush to network before the neighbors. Along with these questions, this chapter suggests strategies to think sanguinely about this perplexing challenge.

There may be no right answers. But districts are learning that there are many wrong answers.

Districts are caught in a stampede to demonstrate that they are

Managing Quandaries

Quandaries

circumstance: awkward situation, catch-22
situation, plight, pickle, pinch, corner, fix,

Quandary

hole, jam, quandary, dilemma, predicament
dubiety: embarrassment, perplexity, bewilderment,
bafflement, nonplus, quandary
predicament: nonplus, quandary, dilemma

conundrum (noun)
in a quandary, in a dilemma, between Scylla and
Charybdis, between a rock and a hard place,
between the devil and the deep blue sea, doubting

Conundrum
question: problem, hard nut to crack, brainteaser,
conundrum, poser, stumper, floorer, mind-boggler,
headache, unsolved mystery, enigma

Source: **Roget's Thesaurus**

modern, wired and technologically advanced.

One can waste a huge amount of money and achieve minimal effects upon student learning simply by following the trend setters and the erstwhile salespeople who market Silicon Snake-Oil wherever they go.

There are very few experts . . . just a whole bunch of folks who claim to be. The opportunities for failure and waste are readily available to anyone willing to rush right in (with the neighbors) without giving much thought to student learning or purpose.

The educational landscape is currently littered with the growing wreckage of technology projects which arrived with plenty of gleam and plenty of polish but very little value.

Districts are caught in a stampede to demonstrate that they are modern, wired and technologically advanced. What matters in these stampedes is not how the technology is used to improve student learning. What matters is the speed of the network and the number of desktops that can connect with the Internet.

Managing Quandaries

> **Keeping up with the Joneses 2**
>
> This may be a time when it is better not to be first on the block. Given the rapid pace of hardware obsolescence, it may make sense to skip over an entire generation of computers. We could invest the savings in professional development . .
>
> Graffiti scribbles discovered next month in apocryphal graduate school of education hallway.

This rush to network schools is a bandwagon of immense proportions and drastic, recurring costs. The rush may be the most expensive **boondoggle** in the history of American government as politicians rush to put a PC in every classroom just as the French once promised a chicken in every pot.

> **Boondoggle** (noun)
> Unnecessary,wasteful, and often counterproductive work.
> Source: **American Heritage Dictionary**
>
> **Boondoggle**
> be busy: chase one's own tail, boondoggle, waste effort
> be foolish: go on a fool's errand, go on a wild-goose chase, waste effort
> be superfluous: labor the obvious, take a sledgehammer to crack a nut, break a butterfly on a wheel, hold a candle to the sun, waste effort
> misuse: misapply, use a sledgehammer to crack a nut, waste effort
> act foolishly: go on a fool's errand, waste effort
> Source: **Roget's Thesaurus**

Managing Quandaries

The trouble is that we do not really know what we are doing when we network schools. We are not at all clear about purpose or method because it is all so new. We have very few models of good practice and almost no data or evidence to guide decision-making. What little data we have is often tainted by vendors and publishers' self interests and profit motives.

Some would have us believe that it is enough to be networked, as if connectedness were some state of Grace.

Speaking at NECC'97, Bill Gates likened (without any apparent irony) the current networking phenomenon to the Gold Rush of the 1840s. He either lacked knowledge of history, or he hoped that the audience did, since a large percentage of the miners found little more than fool's gold and returned home empty handed. Some of the most impressive profits were achieved by those who fed and housed and equipped the speculators.

Will the rush to network schools prove equally disappointing? Will the biggest profits be realized by Gates and his techno-brethren?

The answer to this question depends, in part, upon the ability of schools to ask the right questions, make the right plans, reserve funds for professional development and think before they leap.

1. Quality vs. Quantity

What is the real cost of buying "cheap" computers?
Many districts sacrifice quality in order to buy more desktops. In order to increase the number of computers available for our students, they scoop up the latest "bargains."

In a period of rapid improvement (and obsolescence) in the speed and capacity of computers, there are always "bargains" available for schools willing to buy last year's model this year. Even though these units will soon function at less than half the speed of current units, the 30 per cent cost savings may make it possible to put three computers in every classroom rather than just two!

Few leaders buying "bargain" computers seem to weigh the true cost of installing computers operating at half speed.

Which is better? Two fast computers capable of running today's and tomorrow's software or three slow computers running at half speed which will be unable to cope with the latest system "enhancements" and "upgrades" within 18-25 months?

The best strategy is to buy a mixture of computers to provide balance. For basic operations, un-networked, inexpensive units like Alpha-Smarts make great sense. For more complicated and demanding tasks, it is better to invest in quality even if the price is dear. The true cost cannot be figured by price tag alone. We begin with function and then buy the units that will accomplish our goals.

2. Hardware vs. Human Infrastructure

What is the right balance of spending between people and equipment?

The greatest single failure of networking school districts is the underfunding of professional development.

While the state of Illinois now requires that 25% of any technology budget is devoted to staff learning, most states remain silent on that subject and most districts commit few dollars to prepare teachers for use of the network.

Evidence keeps mounting that a very large number of the new networked computers will go unused unless districts provide 15-60 hours of professional development opportunities yearly so that teachers can turn around and blend these new tools into the daily life of their classrooms.

This professional development challenge is not a simple matter of teaching applications and software skills. We cannot simply provide Internet 101, Internet 102 and Internet 103.

We must all do a better job of explaining to school board members, community members, superintendents and others the risks of underfunding such efforts. We must point to the glowing screens of unused computers and make the consequences clear.

To network a district without a full commitment to professional development is a waste of taxpayers' money and a dramatic drain of scarce resources away from critically important alternatives such as library books, art programs, decent class size and many other programs which are often shortchanged in order to fund the omnivorous technology beast.

Networking well can create impressive gains in student learning. Networking badly is a bit like picking up a drug habit.

3. Skill & Drill vs. Information Power & Literacy

What is the best use of technology?

Since no one ever seems to have enough computers, we find ourselves having to set priorities. If a student can only hope for 2-4 hours of computer contact time weekly, what would be the most profitable use of those hours? If she or he were lucky enough to enjoy

6-10 hours each week, what would be the most profitable use of those hours?

In some places the equipment and the labs are just about fully scheduled with instructional software that promises improved test scores. These districts should not waste any money networking and connecting to the outside world because students are rarely allowed access to the computers for anything approaching exploration or research.

In other districts, there is a ban on the use of drill and practice software in favor of student writing, research, and problem-solving, tapping the network to gain access to rich information which is analyzed with powerful software tools.

Skill and drill programs are the easiest to install and maintain. They require little from the regular teachers. But they represent a major impediment for the classroom teachers who welcome the arrival of networked information resources as a boon to support student thinking. It is also doubtful whether such instructional software will produce the benefits claimed.

Even though some would argue that we network in order to give our children access to the world outside the brick walls of our schools, some of the districts with the most impressive networks have remarkably little traffic going either in or out of the district. They are too intent on drilling and skilling to allow for exploration. And they are often too fearful to allow students access to either information or e-mail.

A network that is heavily filtered and heavily restricted is something like a golden playpen.

4. Short Term vs. Long Term

How long can we continue to budget year to year?
Many leaders ignore the true costs of the project and ignore the necessity of replacing computers every three years. They have no plan (or funding) to make sure that outmoded computers are replaced in a timely fashion. In many districts, the superintendent who launches the network leaves before the first wave of computers makes it through their third year.

"Let the next guy worry about it."

When we add computers to a network, we seriously reduce their life expectancy. It is not that they actually slow down and die more rapidly. The network software and applications software programs simply demand more and more speed and hard drive space from the participating computers.

Most districts act as if they think the initial installation of the network and PCs is the beginning and the end of the project. Very few provide a comprehensive plan mapping out the routine and systematic replacement of all desktops once they have ceased to pull their weight on the network.

Unfortunately, there are too many districts that networked a few years back and now find themselves rusting because they fear the risks attached to asking the local citizens for more money. The same districts with no plan for replacement of outmoded equipment are also unlikely to have set aside adequate sustained funding to make sure the professional development and technical support is there to grow a robust program which is thoroughly infused.

A related problem is the failure to hire a large enough staff of technicians and network professionals to "develop" the network, adding resources, software and various updates to the system as the teaching staff calls for an increasingly rich menu of information and problem-solving tools.

Without adequate staffing, networks hum along with little traffic and little utility as each request for installation of new resources causes a crisis and aggravates an already excessive workload.

"Can't be done!" echoes through far too many hallways and conference rooms.

It makes little sense to introduce a complex network and then leave it unsupported and struggling.

5. Technology as Goal vs. Technology as Path

What is our real purpose?

Some of us have been saying for some time now that this is about information, not technology, but there are many network designers and technology experts for whom the technology is an end in itself.

In many places, the network becomes the goal. Until the district is wired, being wired is the Holy Grail. In some states business leaders and legislators join in arguing that networking is the path to a golden future, that the modern work place needs technologically literate workers.

The trouble is that the mere existence of a network does not prepare students for the work place. If they never get to use the network for problem solving and communication like their work place counterparts, they will remain technologically illiterate even while sitting within range of a great network.

Once the network is installed, we realize that it is simply a path or vehicle to carry us to our true destination. We must make it clear that installation of the network is only the beginning of a long journey. What matters is what we allow students to do with all of this information and communication power.

6. Network vs. Content

What is the right stuff?
We need to balance the needs of the network with the desire to offer powerful tools, rich information, and robust communication to both staff and students.

The fastest and smoothest operating networks are the ones with little traffic and use. Heavy traffic and use may undermine stability and performance. It is tempting, therefore, for network professionals to discourage some of the proposals of teachers and educators who might be inclined to promote heavy use of the network in the service of learning.

Student e-mail is one of the most glaring examples of this conflict. Across North America we are seeing huge networks installed which might support global e-mail exchanges and projects. The potential is enormous.

But . . . In all too many districts the network professionals will fight against student e-mail accounts, using every excuse from workload to Internet abductions as a reason to prohibit student accounts.

Imagine buying a Rolls Royce and keeping it in the garage!

7. Equity vs. Focus

How can we share resources most fairly with maximal impact?
In the name of equity, some schools spread their new technology resources out so thinly as to undermine their impact on the school program.

The danger in handing out the resources equally to all lies in the resulting dilution of program effects. Without a critical mass of computing and information resources, there is little chance that teachers will be able to make significant use of what they are given.

It is a supreme irony that fairness, in this case, can prove deeply unfair to the children. We must look for ways to cluster and combine and move the resources about so that fairness and the curriculum are both well served.

142

Managing Quandaries

8. Lab vs. Distributed

Where will the technology do the most good for the most students in the most integrated manner?
We ought to put the computers where they will do the most good. Doing so requires customized design. In too many districts, someone arbitrarily selects one strategy or the other and imposes it willy-nilly on all the buildings throughout the district . . .

Some put all their computers in labs. Others spread them out with a few in each classroom. The wisest decision-makers put computers and other technologies where they will accomplish the most good for the most students. They have some labs of 30, some labs of 15, some groupings of 10, some flotillas and some classrooms with 6-8 computers used daily in support of the curriculum.

Student learning governs the invention and design process. Over time, we move from centralized collections toward more distributed arrays as staff and students both acquire the skills and the propensity to employ these tools daily in all of their work.

9. Fixed vs. Flexible

What is the best way to protect against rapid change and surprise?
When we are sailing uncharted waters or when we are exploring new regions, we need to beware of certainties and bolts.

Since we have little real experience with wired classrooms, we should be careful about bolting anything down to the floor or into the walls. To prepare ourselves for the inevitable changes we will demand once we try out the equipment and then new resources, we must give flexibility a great deal of weight as a planning value.

Open mindedness is essential in times of rapid change and uncertainty. Rigid plans and liberal pouring of concrete undermines our ability to dart and weave and change course as we see what lies ahead.

10. Closed vs. Open

How can we be safe but not sorry?
The security of a network requires that some aspects be locked down. A totally open system would allow serious damage as well as invasions of privacy and other information crimes.

At the same time, overly rigid notions of security can seriously undermine the value of the network to the end users and clients. The cry of "security" can be used to block very important educational ventures.

The healthiest networks balance the need for security with an appreciation of the benefits which can flow from a reasonably open system.

11. Internal vs. External Expertise

What is the best way to learn what to do?

The first time a district installs a big network, they probably do not have many skilled and experienced insiders to do the design and installation. This lack of inside expertise leaves districts vulnerable to several dangerous traps.

Trap One - MegaBytes & MegaBucks

Hire an outside consulting firm that may design and install a network without much understanding of how new technologies should be used by children. These firms are often highly skilled at laying cable and installing networks but clueless when it comes to schooling and learning. They design networks that do not belong in schools. They connect all the classrooms and the schools with the biggest and the best infrastructure possible.

Long before the technologies arrive, these firms are hardwiring districts for streaming video and other razzle-dazzle technologies that are usually well around the corner.

Like a bad heart transplant, these networks will be rejected by teachers who have something important (called "schooling") to do.

Antidotes:

- Make sure the design firm prominently involves classroom teachers as partners in the firm and as partners in the design process. Student learning should be paramount in their design process.
- Request a list of all school district clients from prospective firms and conduct site visits to see if the claims of the design firm hold up to scrutiny.
- Send half a dozen staff members to network design classes so they can double-check the recommendations of the outside firm.
- Hire a highly respected but independent networking consultant to do nothing but critique the suggestions of the design firm.

Trap Two - Empire Within

Hire a skilled networking design engineer/supervisor from the business world as a district manager and give this new person (who rarely understands classrooms) more power than any of the curriculum savvy district administrators such as the supervisor of libraries or the director or curriculum. Further isolate this leader from curriculum priorities by having her or him report to the business administrator rather than a curriculum person.

Antidotes:
- Make sure that all network professionals report as a department to an administrator whose primary role is curriculum leadership.
- Do not grant network professionals veto power or control over vital curriculum-related decisions.
- Hold them accountable to quality and service issues drawn from the work of Deming and others.
- Make it clear that schools are about learning and that networks are installed to serve clients . . . students and teachers.
- Do not allow network professionals to operate independently from their client base.

Trap Three - Nobody Knows

Lacking local talent and expertise is no barrier for some districts. They go right ahead and promote a staff member from within with no prior experience to oversee the design and installation of the network. They figure this local staff member will be able to learn on the job.

If a district settled on this strategy two years before installation and invested heavily in the education of the new leader, this strategy might have some value. Given enough time and enough field visits to see who is successful, an internal leader might emerge capable of shaping the network to match district needs.

Unfortunately, the selection process is usually conducted within days (if not hours) of the installation itself, and the candidate is rarely given much in the way of training or preparation.

References

Arfman, J. and Roden, P. (1992) "Project Athena: Supporting Distributed Computing at MIT." **IBM System Journal**, v. 31, n. 3, pp. 550-563.

ASLA and AECT. (1998) **Information Power: Building Partnerships for Learning.** Chicago: American Library Association.

Atwell, N. (1998) **In the Middle: New Understandings about Writing, Reading, and Learning.** Boynton/Cook Publishing.

Barron, Dan. **Information Literacy: Dan's Generic Model.** University of South Carolina.

Becker, Henry. **Internet Use by Teachers**. 1999. http://www.crito.uci.edu/TLC/FINDINGS/internet-use/startpage.htm

Bloom, B. (1954). **Taxonomy of Educational Objectives. Handbook I: Cognitive Domain**. New York: Longmans, Green & Co.

Brooks, M. and Brooks, J. (1993) **In Search of Understanding: the Case for Constructivist Classrooms**. Alexandria, VA: ASCD.

Brown, J. and Duguid, P. (2000) **The Social Life of Information.** Cambridge: Harvard Business School Press.

Bruner, Jerome. (1990) **Acts of Meaning**. Cambridge: Harvard University Press.

Caldwell, Roger L. **Anticipating the Future** http://ag.arizona.edu/futures/ swes 450

Calkins, L. (1994) **The Art of Teaching Writing.** Portsmouth, NH: Heinemann.

Chubb, J. E., & Moe, T. M. (1990). **Politics, Markets, and America's Schools**. Washington, D.C.: The Brookings Institution.

CIO Magazine. (1998) "Desperate Times, Creative Measures." January 1.

Cuban, L. (1986). **Teachers And Machines: The Classroom Use of Technology Since 1920**. New York: Teachers College Press.

Cuban, L. and Kirkpatrick, H. "Computers Make Kids Smarter— Right?" **TECHNOS Quarterly For Education and Technology**, Vol. 7, No. 2, Summer, 1998. http://www.technos.net/journal/volume7/2cuban.htm

Culham, Ruth and Spandel, Vicki. **The Six Traits Writing Model**. Materials available from the NWREL at http://www.nwrel.org/eval/writing/products.html

Davis, Stan. (1997) **Future Perfect.** Perseus Press.

Deal, Terrence E. and Peterson, Kent D. (1998) **Shaping School Culture : The Heart of Leadership.** San Francisco: Jossey-Bass Publishers.

References

Dewey, John. (1916) **Democracy and Education**. Reprint edition, Vol 009 (October 1985,) Southern Illinois University Press.

Eberle, Bob. (1997) **SCAMPER**. Prufrock Press.

Eisenberg, M. and Berkowitz, R. (1990). **Information Problem-Solving: The Big Six Skills Approach to Library and Information Skills Instruction**. Abblex Publishing: Norwood, NJ.

Fenton, Edwin. (1966) **Teaching the New Social Studies in Secondary Schools: An Inductive Approach**. New York: Holt, Rinehart, and Winston.

Friedman, M. (1962). **Capitalism and Freedom**. Chicago: University of Chicago Press.

Fullan, Michael G. (1991) **The New Meaning of Educational Change**. New York: Teachers College Press.

Fullan, Michael G. (1996) **What's Worth Fighting for in your School.** New York: Teachers College Press.

Goodlad, J. (1984) **A Place Called School**. Hightstown, NJ: McGraw-Hill.

Harvey. S. (1998) **Non-Fiction Matters: Reading, Writing and Research in Grades 3-8.** York, ME: Stenhouse Publishing.

Harvey, S. and Goudvis, A. (2000) **Strategies that Work: Teaching Comprehension to Enhance Understanding.** York, ME: Stenhouse Publishing.

Henley, S. and Thompson, H. (2000) "Essential Components of Information Literacy: THE RESEARCH PROCESS," Libraries Unlimited.

Hodas, Steven. (1993) "Technology Refusal and the Organizational Culture of Schools ." **Education Policy Analysis Archives**, http://olam.ed.asu.edu/epaa/v1n10.html

Hyman, R. (1980). "Fielding Student Questions." **Theory into Practice**; 1, pp. 38-44.

INFOZONE from the Assiniboine South School Division of Winnipeg, Canada http://www.mbnet.mb.ca/~mstimson/

Joyce, Bruce R. and Weil, Marsha. (1996) **Models of Teaching.** Needham Heights, MA: Allyn & Bacon.

Joyce, B. (Ed.) (1990) **Changing School Culture through Staff Development**. Alexandria, VA: ASCD.

Keene, E. and Zimmerman, S. (1997) **Mosaic of Thought: Teaching Comprehension in a Reader's Workshop.** Portsmouth, NH: Heinemann.

Langford, Linda. "Information Literacy: A Clarification" in **School Libraries Worldwide**, Volume 4, Number 1.

Learning for the Future: Developing Information Services in

References

Australian Schools (1993) Melbourne, Victoria: Curriculum Corporation.

Lieberman, Ann and Miller, Lynne. (1999) **Teachers—Transforming Their World and Their Work**. New York: Teachers College Press.

Lieberman, A. (1995) **The Work of Restructuring Schools: Building from the Ground Up**. New York: Teachers College Press

Loertscher, David. **The Organized Investigator -** (Circular Model) California Technology Assistance Project, Region VII's web site http://ctap.fcoe.k12.ca.us/ctap/Info.Lit/infolit.html

Loertscher, David. (2000) **Taxonomies of the School Library Media Program**. San Jose: Hi Willow Research & Publishing.

Mandinach, E. and Cline, H. (1992). "The Impact of Technological Curriculum Innovation on Teaching and Learning Activities." Paper presented at AERA.

Mandinach, E. and Cline, H. (1994). **Classroom Dynamics: Implementing a Techology-based Learning Environment**. Hillsdale, NJ, Lawrence Erlbaum Associates, Publishers.

McClintock, Robbie. (1999) **The Educators Manifesto: Renewing the Progressive Bond with Posterity through the Social Construction of Digital Learning Communities**. Institute for Learning Technologies -Teachers College, Columbia University http://www.ilt.columbia.edu/Publications/manifesto/

McKenzie, Jamie. (2000) **Beyond Technology: Questioning, Research and the Information Literate School**. FNO Press. http://fno.org/beyondtech.html

McKenzie, Jamie. (1999) **How Teachers Learn Technology Best**. Bellingham, WA: FNO Press. http://fnopress.com

McKenzie, Jamieson. (1993) **Power Learning**. Newbury Park, California: Corwin Press.

Mendels, Pamela. "Survey Finds Teachers Unprepared for Computer Use." **New York Cybertimes**, September 8, 1999.

Murphy, Carlene and Lick, Dale. (1998) **Whole-Faculty Study Groups: A Powerful Way to Change Schools and Enhance Learning.** Newbury Park, CA: Corwin Press.

A Nation at Risk. (1983) http://www.ed.gov/pubs/NatAtRisk/

NCREL (North Central Regional Educational Lab). (1995) **Plugging In.**

Neuhauser, Peg C. (1993) **Corporate Legends and Lore: The Power of Storytelling as a Management Tool**.

Pappas, Marjorie and Tepe, Ann. **Pathways to Knowledge**, Follett's Information Skills Model. http://www.pathwaysmodel.com/

Postman, Neil and Weingartner, Charles. (1969) **Teaching as a Sub-**

References

versive Activity. New York: Delacorte Press.

Problems of Readiness and Preparation, The September, 1999 report of Market Data Retrieval.

Schwartz, Peter. **The Art of the Long View: Planning for the Future in an Uncertain World**. 1991. New York: Doubleday.

Shenk, David. **(**1997) **Data Smog.** New York: Harper Edge.

Senge, P. (2000) **Schools That Learn: A Fifth Discipline Fieldbook for Educators, Parents, and Everyone Who Cares About Education.** New York: Doubleday.

Sizer, Theodore. (1984). **Horace's Compromise**. Boston: Houghton Mifflin Company.

Stabler, Hank. (1999) "Staffing for Technology Support." Arizona Technology in Education Alliance white paper at http://www.aztea.org/resources/whitepaper/staffing.htm.

Taba, Hilda. (1988) "A Conceptual Framework for Curriculum Design," **Curriculum: An Introduction to the Field**, ed. James R. Gress. Berkeley, CA: McCutchan Publishing Corporation, pp. 276-304.

Tapscott, Don. (1998) **Growing Up Digital.** New York: McGraw-Hill.

Technology Counts '99. Education Week, 1999. http://www.edweek.org/sreports/tc99/articles/summary.htm

Toffler, A. (1990). **Power Shift**. New York: Bantam Books.

Trotter, Andrew. "Preparing Teachers For the Digital Age." **Technology Counts '99. Education Week**, 1999. September 23, 1999. http://www.edweek.org/sreports/tc99/articles/teach.htm

Tucker, R. (1991). **Managing the Future: 10 Driving Forces of Change for the '90s.** New York: G. P. Putnam's Sons

Vaill, Peter. (1989) **Managing as a Performing Art.** San Francisco: Jossey-Bass.

Van Dam, Jan. "Total Cost of Ownership." **Technology and Learning**. October, 1999.

Windschitl, Mark. "The Challenges of Sustaining a Constructivist Classroom Culture." **Phi Delta Kappan**, June, 1999, p. 751.

Wyatt, Edward. "Encyclopedia Green; The High Road at a High Cost.," **New York Times**, October 24, 1999.

1. Is there a sense of purpose? A plan?
    excellent (5) good (4) fair (3) weak (2) poor (1)
    Related Questions: Is there a written district technology plan that clarifies philosophical commitments and directions for district staff? Does this plan focus upon the horizon - the long view? Does it leave room for steering and flexibility as staff learns through experience? Does it address all critical elements of program implementation including staff development as well as hardware purchases? Is the plan research-based? Were all key constituents involved in creating the plan? Does the plan focus on curriculum standards?

2. Are technologies being used?
    excellent (5) good (4) fair (3) weak (2) poor (1)
    Related Questions: Does the district have some method to quantify or track the per cent of time that equipment is being used by staff, students or community members? Is there a system to figure out which staff members are making use of the equipment and which are not? Does the administration and the Board take a position with regard to computer and technology usage? How much usage would be desirable? 100% of the school day? 75%? 65%? 35% 15%? Is there a gap between desired and actual? Does anyone know why? Is there a staff plan to narrow the gap?

3. Are technologies blended into regular classroom learning with an emphasis on literacy and standards?
    excellent (5) good (4) fair (3) weak (2) poor (1)
    Related Questions: If technologies are basic tools for managing information in an Age of Information, they should be used broadly, within the art classrooms, the English classrooms, the vocational classrooms, and all others. Studies of schools have shown that technology usage is often centered in special niches and departments such as a computer department or the media center, and the usage is often concentrated in the hands of a narrow group of pioneers or champions. Are appropriate uses of technologies written into all of the district curriculum documents as mandatory activities to prepare students for the next century? Do all subject teachers make use of on-line databases, CD-ROMs, and word-processing along with print materials for research projects, for example? Do students learn to create multimedia reports?

Appendix A

4. Does the use of technologies mirror workplace realities?
excellent (5) good (4) fair (3) weak (2) poor (1)
Related Questions: Has your district explored how adult workers are currently using new technologies to do scientific research, writing, planning, designing, evaluating, etc.? Has that exploration been translated into school experiences and programs? Is technology thought of primarily as a teaching tool or as a problem-solving tool of every day life? How well are the school technology experiences preparing students for the Information Age workplace and community? Is there an explicit district definition of the Information Age? Is staff aware of how the use of information is transforming work and the kinds of skills required by today's workers? Are technologically savvy representatives of the profit and not-for-profit sectors consulted when the district does technology planning?

5. Is the staff adequately prepared to use the technology?
excellent (5) good (4) fair (3) weak (2) poor (1)
Related Questions: Has the Board funded a comprehensive staff development plan over 3-5 years or more to provide all teachers with sufficient technology skills to implement an appropriate program? Are twenty-five per cent of the technology funds dedidcated to professional development? Does each teacher participate in 15-60 hours of adult learning annually? Are all teachers required to acquire such skills? Are assessment plans in place to determine what course offerings need to be added in future years? Does staff development take place during the regular work year/day or is it added on in ways that require teachers to subsidize the learning with volunteered time? Is compensation for training/learning reasonable and fair?

6. Does the staff ever visit the workplace?
excellent (5) good (4) fair (3) weak (2) poor (1)
Related Questions: What provisions are made for staff members to spend time in the modern workplace seeing how technologies are employed? What percentage of English teachers, for example, have spent a day in a modern newspaper office seeing how technologies support the writing, design, layout, and production of a newspaper? How many science teachers have visited a modern science lab to see how computers may be used to conduct experiments and model scientific phenomena? How many media specialists have visited modern libraries offering cutting-edge information systems?

7. Is access to technology equitable?
excellent (5) good (4) fair (3) weak (2) poor (1)

Related Questions: Does the district monitor technology usage by gender, race, location, and academic track to make certain that access is equitable? What kinds of data are collected and reported to help guarantee equal access? When evidence arises that there are gaps of various kinds, what provision is made to close such gaps?

8. What kinds of relationships should students have with machines?
excellent (5) good (4) fair (3) weak (2) poor (1)

Related Questions: Has the Board expressed community values in concert with the professional staff with regard to desirable relationships between students and machines? Are these values communicated explicitly in Board policy or in a district technology plan? How much time should students be engaged with various kinds of technologies? Who should be in control, the student or the machine? What are the long term consequences of such relationships? How do they relate to other educational goals such as citizenship and self esteem?

9. What implicit values are taught by technologies?
excellent (5) good (4) fair (3) weak (2) poor (1)

Related Questions: Is there a system in place to review the implicit values or hidden curriculum taught by various technologies? If computer software rewards students for correct responses by providing game time or opportunities to blow up aliens, for example, is such a reward system consistent with Board policies and community values? Does the technology stress extrinsic or intrinsic rewards? Is responsibility for reviewing such issues clearly identified? Is there a Board policy regarding software piracy, violations of copyright, and advertising? Do students see ethical behavior modeled by the professional staff? Are ethical issues related to technologies addressed by curriculum areas such as social studies? Are students taught critical thinking and critical viewing skills to equip them to counter propaganda and media distortions? Will they emerge from schooling as thoughtful consumers or impulsive consumers? Will they be passive viewers or active viewers?

10. Does these technologies enhance self-esteem, independence, and imagination?

excellent (5) good (4) fair (3) weak (2) poor (1)

Related Questions: **Workplace Basics** states the need for workers who know how to learn independently, come up with novel solutions to problems, and ride through the turbulence of a changing economy and society with self-confidence and adaptability. Are district technology experiences designed to deliver that kind of workforce? How do you assess progress toward such goals? Do you measure student self-esteem? independence? imagination? Is there a program review process to determine which learning experiences are most likely to promote the growth of such qualities?

11. Is the technology more effective than alternative strategies?

excellent (5) good (4) fair (3) weak (2) poor (1)

Related Questions: Are these technologies the best ways to provide a particular learning experience such as mastering various reading skills? If not, do the technologies deliver results that are superior to corresponding alternatives for a comparable investment? If a district chose to invest in staff development aimed at improving teachers' reading instruction, for example, would students in those classrooms make smaller or larger gains than those in classrooms where an ILS (Integrated Learning System) was installed? Does the district introduce such programs as pilots allowing for compare-and-contrast reviews of costs and benefits? Is the data from such studies made available to the Board as part of the district decision-making process?

12. Is the district evaluating what is happening?

excellent (5) good (4) fair (3) weak (2) poor (1)

Related Questions: What kinds of data are gathered to assess the impact of various technologies? Is the data gathered in an objective fashion following accepted principles for experimental design to avoid bias? Does the evaluation design take into account issues such as the *Hawthorne Effect* and the differential impact of volunteers as implementers of pilot programs? Is data used formatively, as a guide to future decisions and program modifications?

13. Is the technology efficient, flexible, adaptable, and current?

excellent (5) good (4) fair (3) weak (2) poor (1)

Related Questions: Are issues such as processing speed, expandability, and connectivity addressed in district planning and purchasing? If students will be using the technology to do graphics or CAD, for example, do cost considerations result in the purchase of low speed technology that will require students to sit and stare at the screen for minutes at time, wasting thousands of hours over the course of a year? Are models with maximal expandability and adaptability selected to protect against premature obsolescence? Is obsolescent existing technology maintained far past program usefulness because it has not stopped working or broken down? What planning procedures are in place to provide for timely updating of technologies and the transfer of obsolescent equipment to programs where the shortcomings are irrelevant?

14. Do the educators have a strong grip on the technology planning process and the network?

excellent (5) good (4) fair (3) weak (2) poor (1)

Related Questions: Are teachers, librarians, and principals clearly in charge of designing the way the network supports the curriculum and learning? Do those with classroom experience design the user interfaces with children's needs in mind, or do staff with business experience dominate that design process? Do educators have hands-on access to fileservers or are they blocked from access by network staff? Are there sufficient technicians to support robust use of the network? Do the technicians see themselves as supporting the work of teachers?

Total Score____
55-65 = outstanding
45-55 = strong
45 or less indicates a need for improvement

Note: This form may be reproduced without cost or express permission within a school district for planning uses only. All other reproduction, distribution, publishing, or use is prohibited without express permission.

Appendix B - A Future Perfect Scenario

In this scenario, we explore what learning might be like in the future with highly intelligent hand-held computers acting as tutors and learning assistants.

Amy and Nakisha, two middle school students, arrive with a team of classmates at the archeological dig site and proceed directly to their assigned square, designated by a grid of string stretching across the remains of what used to be an Iroquois long house.

"Where did we leave off yesterday?" they ask Joe, their hand held computer.

A smiling face appears on the small screen and provides directions. "You were carefully removing soil from your square when you ran out of time. One of your brushes had begun to uncover what looked like a pottery fragment."

The girls nod their heads and bend down close to see if they can still make out the outline of the fragment. "There it is!" exclaims Nakisha, excitedly. She begins brushing around the piece with great care as she has been taught to do by Joe's careful tutoring. As several inches of surface are freed of dust, a faded painting (perhaps of flowers?) begins to emerge.

Amy holds Joe close to the fragment so the computer can scan the image. "Take a look at this painting, Joe, and tell us what you can."

Joe's scanner goes to work and quickly reproduces the image from the pottery shard to its own screen. After a few moments, Joe reports that several similar pieces were located in nearby squares just that morning by two other teams.

"Can you let us see all of the pieces together?"

The girls stare at the fragments and then begin to move them around on the screen like pieces of a jigsaw puzzle, only the computer allows for a three dimensional effect. Gradually, the pieces begin to take on the look of a water jug.

A Scenario

"Can you clean this up and show us from your memory images of other similar pieces found at other sites?"

The girls peer down at the screen and watch the fragments being rearranged, merged and then brightened on the screen before them. The computer shows them what looks like a freshly made jug with a decorative ring of brightly painted flowers. Another five similar pieces appear in a brief slide show narrated by Joe, who explains which tribe created each piece and what features were unique to each piece or tribe's work.

"Can you date this for us, Joe and get a hold of our teacher for us so we can report our findings?"

Mrs. Grimm's face appears on the screen with a grand smile. "Great work, girls! You have added another important piece to the puzzle. Go right ahead and finish the removal of your fragment, following the normal procedure for labeling, boxing and storing. Send a message to the nearby teams so they can profit from your findings. I'll see you in class tomorrow."

Index

Index

F

I

L

M

N

O

P

Index